# Learning Love

a 30 day Devotional
for Wounded Hearts

by Sharon L Letson
and Chris Glatzel

Penny Princess Press ™

Copyright © 2018 – Penny Princess Press™
www.pennyprincesspress.com

All rights reserved. No part of this book may be reproduced in any form or by any means, except for brief quotations for the purpose of review or comment, without written permission of the authors.

Cover art by Angela Crisp. Used by permission. All rights reserved.
www.facebook.com/AngieCrispArt/.

Scripture quotations marked NLT are taken from the *Holy Bible*, New Living Translation, copyright © 1996, 2004, 2015 by Tyndale House Foundation. Used by permission of Tyndale House Publishers, Inc., Carol Stream, Illinois 60188. All rights reserved.

The Holy Bible, Berean Study Bible, BSB
Copyright ©2016, 2018 by Bible Hub
Used by Permission. All Rights Reserved Worldwide.

THE HOLY BIBLE, NEW INTERNATIONAL VERSION® NIV®
Copyright © 1973, 1978, 1984 by International Bible Society®
Used by permission. All rights reserved worldwide.

ISBN-13: 978-1987407174

ISBN-10: 1987407172

## For our children

It has taken us many years to learn these concepts and begin to apply them in our own lives. You have been with us at points on our journeys when we did not know them as well as we do now and may have been the recipients of us acting out of our own places of woundedness, just as we had been with our parents.

We have not taught you love as well as we now realize we should have. We hope that you can now learn it from the One is our best example of what it means to love.

## For our parents

Love was not a part of your vocabulary any more than it was a part of your parents' vocabulary. We understand that and prefer to move forward in relationships grounded in the love of God, rather than live in a place of blaming you for any lack of love we may have felt growing up. We honor you and love what we've inherited from you – a strong work ethic, and a value for living integral and moral lives. Thank you.

# Table of Contents

Forward ……………………………………………..pg 7
Introduction ……………………………………….....pg 9
Day #1 The Garden of Your Mind ………………….pg 13
Day #2 Forgiveness ………………………………….pg 17
Day #3 - Why is Learning Love Important? ……………pg 20
Day #4 – Be Kind, Rewind ………………………… pg 23
Day #5 – Learning Rest ……………………………..pg 26
Day #6 – We All Fall Short ………………………… pg 30
Day #7 – Remain and Respond ……………………… pg 33
Day #8 – Plowing Up Hard Ground …………….. pg 36
Day #9 – Love as The Motivation ………………… pg 39
Day #10 – Love is a Verb ………………………… pg 43
Day #11 – What Lies Do You Believe About Yourself … pg 46
Day #12 – The "I Can't Love Myself" Lie ……………. pg 49
Day #13 – The "I Can't Appreciate My Gifts" Lie …….. pg 52
Day #14 – The "I Have to Hide Who I Am" Lie …. …... pg 56
Day #15 – The "My Feelings Aren't Valid" Lie ……….. pg 60
Day #16 – The "I'm Too Sensitive" Lie …………….. pg 63
Day #17 – The "I'm Not Worth Loving" Lie ………….pg 66
Day #18 – The "I've Wandered Too Far" Lie …………. pg 69
Day #19 – The "I Am Insignificant" Lie ……………… pg 73
Day #20 – The Lie of Recognition vs (In)Significance ….pg 77
Day #21 – The "I Am Invisible" Lie ………………....pg 81
Day #22 – The "Invisible is Safer" Lie ……………... pg 85
Day #23 – The "I Am Unwanted" Lie ……………..... pg 89
Day #24 – Comparison Leads to Jealousy ……………. pg 93
Day #25 – Fear of Failure ……………………………. pg 96
Day #26 – Shame Says You Are Bad ………………….pg 100
Day #27 – The "I Am Unqualified" Lie ……………… pg 104
Day #28 – The "My Thoughts Condemn Me" Lie ……. pg 107
Day #29 – The "My Behavior Condemns Me" Lie …….. pg 110
Day #30 – The "I Am a Victim of My Circumstances" Lie pg 113

# Forward

An emotionally healthy heart is a heart connected to others, but without a good foundation of understanding love, those attempts at connection often fall short and we fail to truly make solid attachments. If that sounds like you then you are in the right place to begin this journey.

As you work your way through this book, we hope to show you how to process some of the hurt and pain that has caused your disconnectedness. We are speaking from a place of experience. Having grown up in a large household with our emotional and physical needs often neglected, we have accumulated our own baggage and issues that we carried into adulthood. We don't claim to have successfully worked through every one of them, but we have made significant strides in the right direction. We know if you genuinely invest yourself in the process that you will as well.

*Sharon Letson and Chris Glatzel*

# Introduction

The title of this book is "Learning Love", not "Learning *to* Love", because we feel that you first must know what love is before you can learn to apply it in any situation. "Learning love" comes from the idea that for those of us who were brought up in households without a solid foundation of love, it is very easy to get confused about what love is. Many of us were never shown love in a tangible way as children. It's impossible to give away something that we don't possess, therefore we first must learn what love is and experience it before we can show it to ourselves and others.

My siblings and I often joke that we were raised by wolves. That is our way of dealing with the reality of our upbringing, which involved a lot of time caring for ourselves. We know now as adults, that our parents did the best they knew how. There just were a lot of kids, which my mother wanted, but my father didn't; a lot of fighting between our parents; a permissive mother who didn't know how to discipline, whose own emotional needs were not met; and an authoritarian father who knew only the value of a hard day's work, who was gone most of the time, but angry when he was there. And if we look back further at the households our parents were raised in we can see why they were that way.

I was 16 the first time I ever heard my father say anything that sounded like 'I love you'. I believe the conversation centered around a relationship I had gotten into that my father was concerned about. (Those of you women with absent fathers will probably be able to relate to looking for love in other male relationships.) My father started out his speech of concern with these words, "You know your mother and I love you".

I was stunned. The statement amazed me. I actually didn't know that my parents loved me, nor did those words feel loving. They felt critical rather than caring. And my father had never said anything remotely like that before. There had been nothing in my life up until that point that would have given me any kind of impression that my father, in particular, loved me. No kisses good night, no bedtime stories, no "love you" as we left for school or even a concerned, "wear your sweater, it's chilly". But there had been plenty of other kinds of messages. Ones that said we were no good, in the way, even unwanted.

So, when I heard messages about God loving us like a father, I didn't have anything to relate it to. And maybe you don't either. Maybe that's why you picked up this book. For people like us who were not brought up in a home grounded in a secure demonstration of love, we need to *learn* what love really means.

*Sharon L Letson*

As adults we all know what we should think, but for most of us there is this residue of junk left from when we were kids that pops up in the most inappropriate places and causes havoc. Sometimes we overreact to circumstances that wouldn't normally warrant the caustic emotions we are having.

That's when we need to dig down and discover the lie behind it and ask Father God to replace it with the truth. Once we have a revelation from God regarding the lie and the truth, we can then begin to be "transformed by the renewing of our mind".

> *Do not conform to the patterns of this worlds thinking, but be transformed by the renewing of our minds. The world's thinking is contrary to God's, so we need to change the way we think. (Romans 12:2, paraphrased)*

Most of those lies exist in our subconscious and come to the surface only occasionally. When they do it's a good opportunity to expose them to the light, to "bring every thought captive." As it says in 2 Corinthians 10:5:

> *We demolish arguments and every pretension that sets itself up against the knowledge of God, and we take captive every thought to make it obedient to Christ. (NIV)*

Dr. Leaf * describes this process in her books and videos, as the mind changing the brain. We have old ugly thoughts that look like trees and when we have a new thought, it takes 21 days to take down and replace the old with the new, and another 21 days to grow the new thought, and another 21 to establish it. So, each time we discover a lie, we are actually renewing our mind! And our brain!

*Chris Glatzel*

\*Dr. Caroline Leaf, <u>Switch on Your Brain</u>

## Day #1 – The Garden of Your Mind
### By Chris Glatzel

Our minds are like gardens. If we plant good seeds, positive things will grow, but too often negative ideas have been instilled in us while we were still very young and little thistles have taken root. Jesus tells a story in Matthew 13 about a farmer who planted good seed in his field, but his enemy planted weeds among the wheat. The weeds grew up alongside the wheat, but the farmer doesn't want his workers to pull out the weeds because it would damage the wheat. He allows both to grow together until the harvest and then they will be sorted out.

When you were a child it could have been very damaging to pull out the negative weedy messages that have gotten planted in your heart and mind. But now that you are mature, and it is time to start cleaning out the weeds. We all need to ask ourselves if there are negative ideas and habits that have grown into the gardens of our minds that we are holding onto instead of pulling.

When I ask myself that question, the answer is yes. I'm slowly but surely identifying the junk that was inadvertently planted in the fertile soil of my young mind. Lies like not feeling welcome when I walked into a room; lies from high school like feeling like I didn't fit in.

Our dad and mom were married young. She was 17 a week and he was 19. We grew up not having much and I always felt like the poor kid. When I got older I always felt "less than" around my friends. Like I was still that poor kid. I realized that feeling was shame. Maybe you have had your own version of shame that has sprouted and grown into your life.

Satan plants lies in the garden of many young minds, and for the rest of your life he reinforces them and continues to make you feel that you aren't important or significant and those lies build up until you are convinced they are the truth.

When we were children, and sometimes even into adulthood we don't always have the correct tools to cope with the thoughts that spill out from all those negative ideas. These ideas could have come from a number of sources like school, siblings, or parents. When I realized that was what was happening to me, I had a choice - to deal with it or not. I chose to deal with it.

These lies that have taken root can wreak havoc in our adult lives and make a mess of things. We sometimes wonder why our lives have gotten so far off course. When we begin identifying the thistles and weeds that have taken root in the gardens of our minds we can start making progress toward a healthier mindset.

When I found myself feeling not good enough, I needed to find the lies, and replace them with the truth. A big clue that you might be believing a lie, is that you are always struggling with significance and self-worth. According to Dr leaf when we try and convince ourselves of something we know in our heads, but it doesn't feel that way in our gut, it is called a cognitive dissonance. Good news, Father God has provided us a way to clean up that mess and address the lies of thistles and thorns. We need to get a revelation of the truth from God and then forgive those that have wounded us.

If you've had shame following you around your whole life, there are steps to get out from under it. Ask God what lie are you believing, and then ask him what the truth is. When He reveals to you what the lie is and then the truth, repent for believing the lie. It's all about agreement. We empower what we agree with, so we need to make sure we are agreeing with the truth and not reinforcing the lies.

Forgiveness and repentance are the spiritual tools He has given us to clean up our messes. It takes 21 days to take down one of those ugly thought trees in our brains. But isn't that great news? In only 21 days, we can change our brain chemistry. Hallelujah! Then another 21 days to grow a new tree of life. So, sit with God for a bit and ask him some questions. When He begins to reveal the truth, continue to confess it until a new thought replaces the old one.

In your quiet time with God ask Him to show you the negative weeds that you need to begin to address. Write those here: _____
_____
_____
_____

Were there any lies that He specifically highlighted as having taken root in your mind? _____
_____
_____

What truths do you need to begin declaring to uproot those lies? _____
_____
_____
_____
_____
_____

**Art prompt:** Find a piece of paper, and some crayons or colored pencils. Take a few minutes and just start scribbling. What a mess right? Now see if there are some pleasing shapes you might fill in. Some might overlap. Making new colors.

Father God wants to do that with our lives. His Holy Spirit fills in the blank spaces left by the tangled web of our thoughts and brings life and creativity to our world.

Write about your experience with the art project. How did it make you feel? What did you create? _____

_____
_____
_____
_____
_____
_____
_____
_____
_____
_____
_____
_____
_____
_____
_____
_____
_____
_____
_____

# Day #2 – Forgiveness
## Chris Glatzel and Sharon L Letson

Both giving and receiving forgiveness is the key to freedom. Without forgiveness, freedom is not possible. Many people have a hard time forgiving those who have deeply wounded and hurt them, because they have a misconception about forgiveness.

You might be feeling something like - it wasn't fair, it wasn't right, they don't deserve it, if you only knew what they did to me, you wouldn't say I have to forgive.

Forgiveness doesn't mean that what someone did to you was right. Forgiveness doesn't mean that they get off without punishment. Forgiveness doesn't mean you give up all rights. Forgiveness is not the same as trust. It doesn't mean you allow the person to continue hurting you. Forgiveness doesn't mean that you are blaming anyone.

But unforgiveness keeps you stuck. It's been said that unforgiveness is like drinking poison and expecting the other person to get sick. It imprisons the person who is holding on to it and doesn't hurt the one who caused the harm. In fact, it often causes bitterness, hatred and anger and blocks the fullness of God in your life.

But the opposite is also true. Forgiveness frees you. It gets you out of the way allowing God to deal with the offender. It relieves you of the burden you have been carrying. And it closes a door, no longer allowing the enemy access to you.

It allows you to say:

"I choose to give grace."

"I chose to let this person go into God's hands."

"I am not going to be their judge."

Forgiveness is a command from the Lord. Because Jesus freely forgave us for all of our sins, we must also freely forgive. Forgiveness is a choice, not a feeling. Forgiveness is vital to deliverance and freedom.

*Make allowance for each other's faults, and forgive anyone who offends you. Remember, the Lord forgave you, so you must forgive others. (Colossians 3:13, NLT)*

We're asking you to make a commitment to forgiving the people who have caused hurt and woundedness in your life. Holding on to resentment will only keep you bitter and broken.

You may know immediately who you need to forgive, but as you go through this process you also may be surprised at who God brings to mind and reveals to you that you still have some unforgiveness toward.

If you feel like this issue will be difficult for you to lay aside, ask God to help you. When we don't have the strength ourselves, God empowers us as we yield it to Him.

Write your prayer about forgiveness here: _____

_____
_____
_____
_____
_____
_____
_____
_____

Sometimes, even when we go through the process of genuinely forgiving people, we still struggle. When that happens we need to go looking for the lie that is attached to the situation. That's what we hope to help you with in the rest of this book.

Optional Art Prompt. If you have art tools - some sort of paint works well, but crayons or colored pencils will do - express with color and lines how it felt to forgive.

# Day #3 - Why is Learning Love Important?
## By Sharon Letson

The Bible tells us that love is who God is. It is his very nature. I John 4:16 tells us:

> *God is love. Whoever lives in love lives in God, and God in him."*

(NIV)

God is love and He is and always has been relational. He has always wanted to interact with humanity through a love relationship. So, to best understand God, and to walk in a deeper, fuller relationship with Him, we must first understand love.

A little further down in the same passage it says:

> *There is no fear in love. But perfect love drives out fear, because fear has to do with punishment. The one who fears is not made perfect in love.*

Without understanding love, our tendency is to live in a place of fear. Fear of failure, fear of what others think, fear of being hurt by others, fear of abandonment, etc. The list could go on and on. Sometimes the voice we hear in our head is a harsh, yelling voice that causes us to shrink back and be afraid. We need to remember that is not the way God speaks to us. He is always gentle and kind even when He's correcting us. He isn't the one giving us a spirit of fear. God is love and that perfect love casts out every bit of fear. When we get grounded in love, understand it, know what it means when God says He loves us like a father, there is something that grows within us. The fear is pushed away, and confidence and boldness replace it.

One of the things we tend to fear is that somehow we have messed this up so badly that we are on the outs with God. That he has become angry with us or so disappointed in our behavior that He can't look at us. But Romans 8 tells us that there is nothing that can separate us from God's love.

> *For I am convinced that neither death nor life, neither angels nor principalities, neither the present nor the future, nor any powers, neither height nor depth, nor anything else in all creation will be able to separate us from the love of God that is in Christ Jesus our Lord (Romans 8:38-39, BSB)*

Nothing can separate us from God's love. Not even us. There is nothing more powerful than a Christian who is confident in who they are and grounded in his or her relationship with God. When we are secure in God's love, we walk in a confidence and boldness that sends demons scattering. But we can't be bold without being secure and we can't be secure without truly entering into a love relationship with God.

What fear do you most identify with? _____

What is your first memory of feeling that fear? Record that here: _____

_____
_____
_____
_____
_____
_____
_____

Who made you feel afraid? _____

Is this a fear you still struggle with? _____

Why do you think that is? _____

_____

_____
_____
_____
_____
_____

Now let's address the negative emotion of fear that entered your heart.

**FORGIVE:** *Father, I choose to forgive* _____ *for making me feel afraid. I know that you didn't intend for me to be afraid. I reject the lie that you are someone I need to fear and declare the truth that You are always trustworthy.*

If you find yourself re-living a painful moment, take some time and ask God to show you where he was at when you first experienced that pain and what he was thinking about you. Write what you feel he is telling you here:

_____
_____
_____
_____
_____
_____
_____
_____
_____
_____
_____
_____

## Day #4 – Be Kind, Rewind
### By Sharon Letson

You may not be old enough to remember these, but there was a time when we used to rent videos from a movie rental store. These are still around, but videos have now become dvd's and with the rise of online movie access sites, their popularity has decreased. But back when we used to rent videos from the video store, the videos came with a sticker that said, "Be Kind, Rewind". The point was when you finished watching the movie you would need to rewind the video so that the next person who rented it would be watching it from the beginning as soon as they popped it into the player rather than from the end where you stopped when you were done watching it.

We're going to apply this old adage to the movie of your life. Up until now your life has been recording its own movie and there have been a lot of plot twists and interesting characters. You've reviewed this movie so many times that you now have the theme song stuck in your head. This theme song encapsulates the messages you have heard over the years. But not all of those messages have been good. Your theme song may go something like this, "I'm a loser and I can't do anything right. I'm a screw-up and made a mess of my life."

It's time for you to "Be Kind (to yourself) and Rewind (the tapes)". That old theme song needs recording over and replaced with a new song. This new theme song will be written from the pages of the Bible and it's all about the wonderful, loving things God has to say about you.

So, your challenge is to find a verse or a passage that really speaks to you and write that in the space provided. I personally like anything with the word "beloved" in it. Beloved means dearly loved. Some synonyms are adored, cherished, treasured, and prized. I love this verse from Deuteronomy 33.

> *"Let the beloved of the Lord rest secure in him, for he shields him all day long, and the one the Lord loves rests between his shoulders." (vs. 12 NIV)*

Once you find your verse, spend time meditating on it. Write it on a sticky note and post it around your house to remind yourself. Memorize it. Make a song out of it and every time those old messages pop into your head, sing it to yourself. It takes a lot of repetition to get the old song that's been programmed in there out of your head and replace it with a new song.

That's what the **REWIND** portion of your devotional is going to be about. We'll help you replace the negative messages you have internalized about yourself with God's truth.

Start by writing down the words to the old theme song of your life's movie. You know, the negative messages that keep popping up that you have so much trouble getting out of your head. Perhaps the negative messages are associated with a particular person: _____

_____
_____
_____
_____
_____
_____
_____

Now, in capital letters write the word LIE over those words. It's time to rewrite that theme song.

**FORGIVE:** *God, I choose to forgive* _____ *for all of the negative things s/he (they) said about me.*

**REWIND:** *I reject those negative characterizations as lies and embrace your truth that I am dearly loved by you.*

Did you find a verse to use for your new theme song? Great! Write that here: _____

_____
_____
_____
_____
_____
_____
_____

# Day #5 – Learning Rest
## by Sharon Letson

**REST** is the next prompt we're going to add to your daily processing. You see we often get stuck in a cycle of doing good things for the wrong reasons. These activities often look like things that we should be doing, but if we look closely we would see feelings of shame, guilt, or performance to gain acceptance as the motivators.

Our earthly father was a hard task master. At least that is the way it seemed to us. He wasn't around much, but when he was, he was diligently teaching us the 'value of hard work' as he used to say. Given that our mother rarely made us do any chores, it was probably a lesson we needed to learn. But unfortunately, it was the only lesson we learned from him. Because praise or acceptance was never given for anything, especially internal traits like kindness, honesty, or consideration for others, we found ourselves unconsciously trying to earn acceptance through performance, because our value as children became tied to what we did, not who we were.

This is where I operated most of my life. The problem was that no matter what I did, I never measured up. I never could will myself to do all the right things, 100% of the time. The first time I got a divorce I felt so worthless. Like many women before me, I looked to relationships to feel loved. But I always picked the guys who were as needy and messed up as I was. You see it's hard to be in a healthy emotional relationship when you aren't emotionally healthy. And it is difficult to do everything right all the time, especially when you don't have the tools you would have gotten through a more loving upbringing.

People stuck in performance mode are more comfortable with a to-do list than with just sitting and interacting with the people around them. Learning to be relational is difficult for this type of person. It takes a lot of practice and determination. Just remember that you are a human *being*, not a human *doing*. Being kind and considerate are much more valuable traits than checking off tasks on your religious to-do list, even when the things on your list are good things.

I love these verses from Matthew 11:28-30.

> *Then Jesus said, "Come to me, all of you who are weary and carry heavy burdens, and I will give you rest. Take my yoke upon you. Let me teach you, because I am humble and gentle at heart and you will find rest for your souls. For my yoke is easy to bear and the burden I give you is light. (NLT)*

Unlike many of our earthly fathers, Father God is not a hard task master. He is not sitting around, waiting for us to prove ourselves to Him. As we can see in these verses, He does not give us heavy burdens. Instead He is partnering with us to help us carry our loads and offers us something amazing – rest!

The picture He gives us is of a yoked pair of oxen. A yoke is a wooden device placed on the neck of two oxen, binding them together. It is placed over both the oxen so that the weight of the load is shared. And when the One who is carrying your burdens with you is the Creator of the Universe, you know He's the bigger, stronger ox who can easily bear the weight of any load, leaving you to rest in your position just trotting along beside him.

There are many other pictures of resting in God that the Bible gives us. Let's look at another one of them. In Psalm 27 the picture becomes of Him concealing or hiding us in a place of protection when we are faced with trouble. It begins in verse 4, but the portion pertaining to rest is in verse 5.

> *The one thing I ask of the Lord — the one thing I seek most — is to live in the house of the Lord all the days of my life, delighting in the Lord's perfections and meditating in his Temple. For he will conceal me there when troubles come; he will hide me in his sanctuary. He will place me out of reach on a high rock.*

In this passage we can see some actions — delighting and meditating - but these are not the normal Christian good deed actions we think of. We think of things like teaching the children's class, singing in the choir, or being in the outreach or visitation ministries. We need to move to a place of delighting and meditating. In other words, rest.

So, any time you find yourself checking tasks off of a religious to-do list, remind yourself that you need to rest. It is too easy to become busy with things that look good — ministry, helping at church, caring for others. Only we don't always realize that we have the wrong motivations for doing those things.

What does that mean for all those good things you're doing? Do you need to stop? Maybe? It might be necessary to reset and stop doing for a while until you learn how to rest in God. Then before accepting any new tasks in your life check your motivation for doing them. Are you choosing to do that thing because you fear someone will be unhappy with you if you don't? Does not doing it make you feel guilty? Does it somehow feel comfortable and safe, because it is over on the list of good things to do? Are you trying to get recognition for the good you do? Or are you responding to the Holy Spirit's prodding? As you learn to walk in relationship with God you will begin to discern the difference.

**FORGIVE:** *God, I choose to forgive myself for trying to earn your acceptance through _____.*

**REWIND:** *I reject the lie that I have to do anything to earn your love.*

**REST:** *I accept the truth that I can just enjoy delighting in you and meditating in your presence.*

Think about all the 'good' things you do. Which of them are you doing for the wrong reasons? _____
_____
_____

Are these things you think you should stop doing? _____
What steps could you take to do that? _____
_____
_____

Who could you ask to help you take these steps? _____
What does resting in God's love for you look like? Feel like? _____
_____
_____
_____
_____
_____
_____
_____

# Day #6 – We All Fall Short
## by Sharon Letson

One day I realized, that the fact that I couldn't measure up was exactly the point. I've fallen short, because we've all fallen short. That's why I need Jesus. That's the whole point! I could never be good enough to somehow make myself acceptable.

There is a cool thing I never noticed in that passage from Romans 3. The whole thing reads:

> *But now a righteousness from God, apart from law, has been made known, to which the Law and the Prophets testify. This righteousness from God comes through faith in Jesus Christ to all who believe. There is no difference, for all have sinned and fall short of the glory of God, and are justified freely by his grace through the redemption that came by Christ Jesus. (Romans 3:21-24, NIV)*

The Jewish law was all about the do's and don'ts. Many of us can relate, because the type of Christianity we grew up with was all about the rules we kept. But God's righteousness is about faith in Jesus, not about keeping laws.

This was an epiphany moment for me. All have fallen short! I was no different than anyone else. And I was no surprise to God. There is no way to be good 100% of the time, simply through sheer will. At least *I* had no ability to do it. But look at the next verse *'all are justified freely by his grace'*.

Amazing! To fall short, simply means we've all made mistakes. But the next verse, which usually gets left out, states that we *all* are justified through Jesus when we've placed our faith in Him! No matter what mistakes we've made!

In Romans 4, it becomes clear that God doesn't look at what we do or don't do to make us right with Him. The passage is speaking of Abraham being the father of those who were made righteous by having the same kind of faith he had. Starting in verse 13 we read:

> *Clearly, God's promise to give the whole earth to Abraham and his descendants was based not on his obedience to God's law, but on a right relationship with God that comes by faith. If God's promise is only for those who obey the law, then faith is not necessary, and the promise is pointless. For the law always brings punishment on those who try to obey it. (The only way to avoid breaking the law is to have no law to break!) So the promise is received by faith. It is given as a free gift. And we are all certain to receive it, whether or not we live according to the law of Moses, if we have faith like Abraham's."*
> *(Romans 4:13-16, NLT)*

No matter what we do, we can't *do* enough to earn acceptance. It requires only faith. So. when we place our faith in Jesus, we receive the free gift of God's promise. Keeping or not keeping the law of Moses will not affect it.

We've seen that failing at life, or 'falling short', is simply part of the human experience. It's time to stop beating yourself up for making those mistakes. In the passage from Romans 4 it says that the only way to avoid breaking the law is if there were no law to break. But we also see that the opposite of living according to the law is living by faith.

Faith, however, is confidence. You can't will yourself to have enough faith. You can't conjure it up. Faith is something that grows as you experience the faithfulness of God. And it will grow as you walk through this process and continue to invite God into it to walk through it with you. As you experience his trustworthiness and learn more of what his love for you looks like and feels like, your faith will increase. You will no longer need to depend only on yourself, because you will have the One who is more reliable than any person could ever be to look to for direction and comfort.

**FORGIVE:** *God, I choose to forgive myself for the mistakes I've made of* _____.

**REWIND:** *I reject the lie that those mistakes have disqualified me in any way from belonging to You.*

**REST:** *I accept the truth that I can live a life of faith, which will continue to grow and develop as I depend on You.*

In what ways have you 'fallen short'? _____

_____

_____

_____

How could you grow your faith through those situations? _____

_____

_____

_____

_____

_____

_____

_____

_____

_____

# Day #7 – Remain and Respond
## by Sharon Letson

This concept of rest is so important that we are going to spend one more day here before we move on. Remember, the idea is that you can't do anything to earn God's love. Instead you must rest in God's love for you. That means you begin to believe it is there without you having to do anything to earn it..

John 15 illustrates this for us. In it Jesus refers to himself as the true grapevine, us as branches, and to his Father as the gardener. Jesus often painted pictures in this way, by pointing to something the people he was speaking to were familiar with and making a spiritual connection. Verse 4 says:

> *"Remain in me, and I will remain in you. For a branch cannot produce fruit if it is severed from the vine and you cannot be fruitful unless you remain in me." (NLT)*

Some translations use words like 'stay connected to' or 'joined to', but the idea is that our actions (fruit) should flow out of our connection to Jesus. The life that is in Him will flow through us out to our actions. We can connect through worship, by talking to him, or by reading His words. Just remember that we're not talking about doing all the right things for all the wrong reasons. Prayer and Bible Study can become as much of a religious habit as anything. Rather than doing it because you have a set number of chapters to read or a set amount of time to pray, try being aware of His presence and of what He's speaking to you through His word. And remember that if the voice you hear sounds condemning and you begin to feel guilty for not doing enough, that is not God.

> *"So now there is no condemnation for those who belong to Christ Jesus. And because you belong to him, the power of the life-giving*

*Spirit has freed you from the power of sin that leads to death."
(Romans 8:1-2, NLT)*

Learning to rest in God takes practice. We encourage you to spend as much time here as necessary. Once you've learned to rest then you need to learn how to **RESPOND**.

I spent my whole life trying to be the good girl, fearing that Dad and by extension Father God would be mad at me if I did anything wrong. But obviously I did plenty of things wrong, especially since I didn't have the tools I needed to have healthy relationships. And it probably isn't fair to say that there weren't any interactions with our father except for the ones where he had a job for us to do, or he was angry or critical of us, but if there were, they were few and far between and I don't remember them. It was after my second divorce that I realized that I was trying to earn God's love through my actions. It was then that I encountered this verse.

*We love because he first loved us. (I John 4:19, NIV)*

That's it. Just one simple phrase. But what a profound statement. Not only could I never measure up – never be able to 'earn' it, not only was I invited to rest in God's love for me, but now I knew that anything I did do needed to be a response to His love.

That looks very different than doing all the good Christian things because I feel guilty if I don't. It means walking in relationship with God. In that relationship I seek wisdom from God before choosing to take on any more Christian tasks. I am not trying to earn His acceptance, instead I respond to His love by loving others, as it says in Romans 5:5 says:

> *"And hope does not disappoint us, because God has poured out his love into our hearts by the Holy Spirit, whom he has given us." (NIV)*

We can't give away what we don't possess. We have to let God show us his love and really 'get it' inside our own spirits before we can try and give it away to others. Ask God to show you how to do that.

**FORGIVE:** *God, I choose to forgive myself for trying to live a good life without connecting myself to you.*

**REWIND:** *I reject the lie that good actions are the same as connecting to you.*

**REST:** *I accept the truth that there is no condemnation in your voice, and that as I learn to stay connected to you that I can respond appropriately by showing the love you have given me to others.*

**RESPOND:** What ways has God shown you that He loves you?

_____
_____
_____
_____

How could you respond to that love? _____
_____
_____
_____

How could you share that love with someone else? _____
_____
_____
_____
_____
_____

## Day #8 – Plowing Up Hard Ground
### By Sharon Letson

We know from experience that this journey of learning what love is and applying it in our lives does not happen overnight. In fact, we still have issues that unexpectedly intrude on our lives, but we are a lot further down the road than we were when we started.

Think of the idea about the truth of God's love for us like that seed we are trying to plant. But in order for our hearts to be ready for that seed of love to be planted, the ground of our hearts may need to be plowed up. Often in response to emotional pain, our hearts grow hard. We let nothing in, because we are afraid that we will get hurt again. Hard bristly, thistles grow, daring anyone to approach, and those that do try to get close to us, pull back, scratched and pierced from the attempt. Most won't stay and try again to reach us, and when they walk away, the idea that we are unlovable is reinforced.

If a hard, crusty layer lays over the ground of your heart, it may have been a legitimate response to deep wounds you received. Those responses have been necessary to protect you, to keep you physically and emotionally safe. But not dealing with that hardness keeps more things out than just pain. It keeps out love – the love of others and of God.

God can be trusted to be gentle with your heart. He will not push you beyond what you can bear. Instead, He will tenderly lead you and grow you into a deeper relationship where you can know you are cared for and loved.

We know this can be difficult, but you don't need to be afraid of the hard places. Think about people in the Bible whose identities were forged in the hard places. Joseph was sold into slavery and eventually spent a lot of years in prison before he became second only to Pharaoh. Moses spent a lot of years on the back side of the wilderness before he became the deliverer of the Hebrews. And little David was the overlooked son of Jesse, who wasn't even considered by his father to be presented to the prophet Samuel when God sent him there to appoint one of Jesse's sons king. He was left out in the fields to tend the sheep. But what did he learn there? He learned to fight off the lion and the bear to protect the sheep. His training out in the fields prepared him to face the giant. These men became the founders of our faith that we look to as examples. Each of them learned about the faithfulness of God in the hard places of life.

We want you to go slowly, because it takes time for a sturdy plant to grow that is 'rooted and grounded in love'. You will go through seasons of plowing, planting, and growing. Trust the process and know that it takes time.

Our prayer for you is this:

*"When I think of all this, I fall to my knees and pray to the Father, the Creator of everything in heaven and on earth. I pray that from his glorious, unlimited resources he will empower you with inner strength through his Spirit. Then Christ will make his home in your hearts as you trust in him. Your roots will grow down into God's love and keep you strong. And may you have the power to understand, as all God's people should, how wide, how long, how high, and how deep his love is. May you experience the love of Christ, though it is too great to understand fully. Then you will be made complete with all the fullness of life and power that comes from God." (Ephesians 3:14-19, NLT)*

Hardness comes from hurt. Think about a hurt that caused your heart to put up defenses. Let's start by dealing with that hurt.

Think about what you are most afraid will happen if you let down the walls you've put up to protect yourself. _____

_____

_____

_____

_____

Ask God to show you where that hardness began to develop. Record that here:_____

_____

_____

What did you believe about yourself, God, or others because of that incident? _____

_____

**FORGIVE:** *God, I choose to forgive* _____ *for* _____.

**REWIND:** *I reject the lie that I am* _____, *and that God is* _____.

**REST:** *I declare the truth that I am* _____ *and that You are* _____.

**RESPOND:** Think about a person you have not allowed past your protective barriers, who did not deserve to be shut out. How could you reach out to that person in a small way and interact with them? _____

_____

_____

_____

# Day #9 – Love as the Motivation
## By Sharon Letson

To begin to learn what love is we need to first understand that love is not necessarily an emotion. Yes, showing and receiving love produces good feelings that are often called *love*, but if we begin to look at the actions that show love, we can begin to wrap our minds around what love is and is not, and be able to recognize loving actions in ourselves and in others.

The best place to look at the actions of love is in I Corinthians 13, which is often called the Love Chapter of the Bible. This chapter begins by telling us that *love* must be the motivation behind our actions. A good description of the motivation of love is wanting the best for the other person. Love is a strong motivator, but so are many other emotions - pride, arrogance, selfishness, control, judgmental attitudes. But any positive motivator, if we look hard enough, should have desiring the best for the other person at its core.

Is it possible to do the right things for the wrong reasons? Absolutely! In this passage there is a list including speaking the languages of angels, prophesying, understanding God's secret plans, having faith, sacrificial giving to the poor or even sacrificing one's life for another, but after every good deed listed is the reminder, *"if I do not have love, I have gained nothing"*.

When I did my student teaching, I had the privilege to teach Drama. What a fun class! There's a game that we would play where we take the same dialogue and change the emotion behind the words. For example, read the dialogue below normally and then I'll suggest a few changes.

*Teenage son:* "Mom! I'm home!"

*Mom: "Oh great, Todd. There's a snack on the table and then I want you to get started on your homework. You have a test tomorrow."*

*Teenage son: "Thanks for reminding for me."*

Hopefully you imagined that scene as a loving exchange between mother and son. Now read it through again, changing the emotion from love to impatience, then try sarcasm, then anger. You can see that it isn't the words, but the emotions behind them that give them meaning.

Or think of the most beautiful oration you've ever heard. For example, the love scene from Romeo and Juliet where Romeo comes upon the sight of Juliet in the window and begins to declare how beautiful she is. You can imagine a young Romeo caught up on the emotion of young love comparing Juliet's beauty to the rising sun. Done well, words can stir deep emotions within us.

Now imagine Romeo saying the same thing, but not really meaning it, his voice dripping with sarcasm. Instead of Juliet responding with love, he more likely would have received a sharp slap across his face.

Words matter. They carry meaning by themselves, but the motivation behind those words carry a deeper meaning. Are we really thinking about the best interest of the other person or are we thinking about how we can wound them, make them feel small or unimportant, or just reacting out of our own impatience at being disturbed? We often think we can convince others to agree with our point of view through debate, but according to Paul, if we do not speak with love, we might as well be standing there with a large pot, banging on it with a metal spoon.

Jesus said there was no greater love than to lay down your life for a friend. We've seen many such acts of sacrifice in our country when the life of a loved one or even a stranger was threatened. Someone stepped in and selflessly became a barrier between danger and another person, and their life ended. That is an act of love.

It is difficult to consider that a person would give up their life for any other motivation than selfless love, but verse 3 offers another motivation – pride.

> *If I gave everything I have to the poor and even sacrificed my body, I could boast about it; but if I didn't love others, I would have gained nothing. (NLT)*

It's almost as if you can hear the person saying, "look how awesome I am for doing what I'm doing".

Verses 1-3 progress from things that do not require much sacrifice to the one thing that requires the ultimate sacrifice, and yet the claim is made that even that sacrifice profits nothing if it is not done in love.

You can probably think of times when someone else's actions toward you were motivated by something other than love. List a few incidents where someone's motivation was very different than their actions (for example, sarcastic comments): _____

_____
_____
_____
_____
_____

**FORGIVE:** *God, I choose to forgive* _____ *for demeaning me with their words and actions.*

**REWIND:** *I reject the lie that I am defined by them*

**REST:** *I declare the truth that I can be motivated by your love in my actions towards others.*

**RESPOND:** Who did you think of in the first prompt? _____
_____
Is this a person who is still in your life? _____
Try writing a (loving) response to them and let them know how their words and actions have hurt you and how you are choosing to forgive them. _____
_____
_____
_____
_____
_____
_____
_____
_____
_____
_____

It isn't necessary to actually send the note, because it is the process of expressing yourself that is important, but if you feel it is safe to communicate with that person, give it a try. If this person is still in your life and it is not safe, you may need to seek help in separating yourself from them.

# Day #10 – Love Is a Verb
## By Sharon Letson

We said that love isn't necessarily an emotion, therefore love isn't measured as much by how we feel as it is by what we do. Sometimes we get caught up in not feeling loved that we forget to look for the things that are being done in an attempt to demonstrate love. First Corinthians 13 has some helpful descriptions of what love is that we can take some hints from.

*Love is patient, love is kind. (vs 4a, BSB)*

and

*Love… rejoices in the truth. It bears all things, believes all things, hopes all things, endures all things. (vs 6b-7, BSB)*

This list is a good guide for identifying the actions of love. When we are patient with our children, when we show kindness to a stranger we are showing love. When we are impatient or unkind, that is the opposite of love. Truth and love are very closely connected. We know that truth (spoken in love) sets people free, so it is an act of love to appreciate truth, even when said truth is uncomfortable. Misrepresenting the truth is not a loving act.

Bearing all things, believing all things, hoping all things, and enduring all things makes me think of situations where we are tempted to judge, criticize, and perhaps retaliate towards someone else when they have acted badly towards us. Instead, love calls us to endure the negative actions of others and believe the best of them even when it looks different.

An example of this often happens in relationships. Someone says something that sounds like a putdown. Instead of automatically assuming it was meant negatively, love calls us to believe the best of that person, to recall the good characteristics we know they have. Of course, sometimes they meant it exactly how it sounded, and their intention was to wound us. Loving in these situations can be difficult. But just recall the actions of love – patience, kindness, bearing the wounds, and believing the best for that person.

Conversely, we can learn about what love is by examining what it is not. I Corinthians 13 has a few things to saw on that subject also.

> *Love… does not boast, it is not proud. It is not rude, it is not self-seeking, it is not easily angered, it keeps no account of wrongs. Love takes no pleasure in evil. (vs 4b-6a, BSB)*

So, if my actions are on this list I can be assured that I am not being loving. And if this is the way I am treated by someone else, I know that even if they say they love me, their actions are not those of love.

It's easy to see what love is and is not when we look at this passage. We also know that different people, experience love differently. 5 Love Languages by Gary Chapman identifies words of affirmation, quality time, receiving gifts, acts of service and physical touch as ways people give and receive love differently.

Sometimes we don't feel loved because the person is expressing it in a different 'language' and we aren't seeing it as love. Many wives I know feel very loved when their husbands chip in and help with chores around the house. But if the husband is expressing love physically and that isn't really the wife's love language the message isn't getting across. Understanding our own and others' love languages is a very powerful tool to understand the hurt we may feel, despite the attempt at love that was shown to us.

Understanding these love languages can also help us identify why something wounds us that doesn't wound someone else. For example, siblings who have grown up together and experienced the same mistreatment could be wounded in different ways. If your love language is words of affirmation and you are yelled at, that will hurt worse than if your love language is gifts. Or conversely if you received a lot of gifts, but no one spent time with you, and your love language is quality time that will be just as hurtful.

**FORGIVE:** *God, I choose to forgive* _____ *for not loving me in a way I could receive.*

**REWIND:** *I reject the lie that they purposely intended to wound me*

**REST:** *Thank you that I can learn to express love by showing the actions of love to others.*

**RESPOND:** If you've never thought about the way you experience love, www.5lovelanguages.com has a quiz you can take to discover yours.

What are your primary love languages? _____

_____

What actions feel the most loving to you? _____

_____
_____
_____
_____
_____

What are some practical ways you can express love to others via your love language? _____

_____
_____
_____
_____

## Day #11 - What Lies Do You Believe About Yourself?
### by Sharon Letson

As a child you received subconscious messages from the people in your environment. They have been internalized and are now ingrained in the fabric of who you are. But many of those messages now have you believing lies about yourself. We need to begin weeding out those lies in order for love to have room to grow.

The Bible says the truth will set you free (John 8:32), so if you are not experiencing freedom, what you believe just might not be true. When we believe lies about ourselves we are allowing negative emotions to take root - emotions like shame and guilt. Shame says who you are is bad, rather than your actions need changing.

2 Corinthians 7 paints us a picture of the difference between godly sorrow and guilt and shame.

> *"Godly sorrow brings repentance that leads to salvation and leaves no regret, but worldly sorrow brings death. See what this godly sorrow has produced in you; what earnestness, what eagerness to clear yourselves, what indignation, what alarm, what longing, what concern, what readiness to see justice done." (10-11a, NIV)*

The lies we've internalized are also the way we have disqualified ourselves from the message that God loves us. Somehow even if we believe that God is loving and that He loves the world and everyone in it, we unconsciously think it doesn't apply to us. I don't think we do it intentionally because it isn't logical, but we seem to feel that God really can't have meant that He loves us specifically.

The lies you believe about yourself are part of the package placed within you by the atmosphere you were in growing up. The lies I believed about myself included being unwanted, unimportant, as well as the inability to do anything right. If you knew me as a child, you would have seen a timid and fearful child. I walked pigeon-toed with my head down. I would rather wet myself than speak up and let anyone know that I had to go to the bathroom.

Not every child responds to the same environment in the same way, but I was a very sensitive child, so my response to my unpredictable environment was to retreat. I had a fear of being vulnerable, of being known. I was depressed as a teenager, and preferred invisibility as a young adult. I didn't feel that I had anyone else to rely on to help guide me through life. I made decisions in a vacuum, just hoping they were right and then bearing the criticism that was sure to come when it turned out to be wrong.

Let's begin by identifying the messages you were given as a child. Sometimes these messages were not said precisely in words, but you believed them all the same. Think about the damaging words that were said to you and also about the unspoken messages you received.

*I was told by* _____ *that*
*I was* _____.

*I always felt* _____ *because*
_____
_____
_____.

**FORGIVE:** *God, I choose to forgive* _____
*for making me feel* _____.

**REWIND:** *I reject these messages as lies.*

**REST:** *I declare the truth that You love me. I rest in that love.*

**RESPOND:** Think about the people who hurt you as a child. Are you still in relationship with them? If you could reach out to them (in a safe way) what would you say to them? _____

_____
_____
_____
_____
_____
_____
_____
_____
_____
_____
_____

Remember that forgiveness is not trust. We never want you to place yourself into a situation with a person who is not trustworthy, but if you are able, try communicating some of what you wrote above with that person. If not, ask a friend to go through it with you.

# Day #12 The *"I Can't Love Myself"* Lie
## By Chris Glatzel

I've heard it said that humility isn't thinking less of yourself, instead it's thinking of yourself less. If that's the case then when we focus on how bad we feel we are, or on something that we don't like about ourselves, that's actually the opposite of humility. It's focusing on yourself instead of focusing on others. When we look outward, away from ourselves and see others it's good, but if you don't feel you have something to offer others, that you can be helpful, or supportive, or just caring, that's not good.

I've thought about this lie that I cannot love myself. It seems as if I like who I am then it feels like I'm being self-focused. And if I like myself a lot, I'm not being humble. Maybe you feel like you don't even have permission to like yourself.

There seems to be some unwritten rule that says if you love yourself, that means you are narcissistic or arrogant in some way, but how do you tell the difference between arrogance and confidence? And how do we become confident in who we are or who we were created to be without thinking more of ourselves than we should? The idea comes from this passage in Romans.

> *Because of the privilege and authority God has given me, I give each of you this warning: Don't think you are better than you really are. Be honest in your evaluation of yourselves, measuring yourselves by the faith God has given us. (Romans 12: 3, NLT)*

In the Contemporary English Version it says:

> *Use good sense and measure yourself by the amount of faith that God has given you.*

According to Ellicott's Commentary, in the original language the whole phrase is a play on words. Rather than being 'high-minded' we are to be 'sober-minded. Or in other words "to keep sobriety of mind constantly as the object or ideal towards which all the thoughts and feelings converge".

Philippians 4 helps us understand the ideals which we should keep our thoughts fixed on – what is true, honorable, right, pure, lovely, admirable, things that are excellent and worthy of praise. You have some of those qualities and many of your actions reflect those ideals. It's ok to like those things about yourself.

If you aren't able to do that, you need to ask yourself why you aren't able to say, "Hey I'm pretty great. And I like me." There's a lie attached to the belief that liking yourself is arrogance or pride and not having Godly humility.

Ask God to show you what the lie is. What is the lie and when did you start believing it? _____

_____

_____

_____

**FORGIVE:** *God, I choose to forgive* _____
*For making me feel like I don't have permission to like myself.*

**REWIND:** *I reject the lie that being happy with the person I am, my characteristics, and good qualities is arrogance and pride.*

**REST:** *I know the truth is that I am an awesome person made in your image and reflecting your character.*

**RESPOND:** Which characteristics are you most proud of? _____

_____

_____

_____

I'm a firm believer in self-talk. Sometimes there is no one else around to tell us the things we need to hear, so we have to tell ourselves. Stand in front of the mirror and tell yourself why you are an awesome person. This is a practice you need to repeat daily.

# Day #13 The *"I Can't Appreciate My Gifts"* Lie
By Chris Glatzel

When you get gifts for your birthday, they are yours. Perhaps you've received a new article of clothing, like a shirt, and when you wear it and get compliments on it, you might say, "Thank you, it's a gift."

I think it's the same with the gifts and aptitudes we have from God. If you are good at math, and people comment, all you have to say is, "Thanks, it's a gift", because it truly is. You might have worked hard, but the ability to even accomplish that didn't come from you only. It was a gift. But now it's yours, just like the shirt. You own it. You become it. It becomes you. You are like a plastic water bottle filled with all the things God put in you including Himself. The clearer we become the more the attributes of God can be seen, but he still loves the container, and He doesn't want to be rid of you. It's not less of me and more of Him. It's all of me with all my uniqueness with all of Him inside.

For example, I have often been told that I'm too bossy. However, I've realized in the last few years that I have an administration gifting. I was the oldest of 7 kids, so my younger siblings saw this gifting as bossing them around. Even as adults, if I try to organize them, I get the, "you're not the boss of me" attitude. So, for a long time, I didn't understand that it was a gift, and I tried to suppress it. Once I realized what I was dealing within myself, I could then work on learning appropriate leadership styles.

Another one of my 'gifts is that I have a zillion ideas, sometimes daily, and some people call me a visionary. When my kids were young I had entrepreneurial ideas, one of which included a candy store in our old Victorian house. It would have been perfect, but after a few weeks I decided that I probably didn't want to run a candy store and I dropped the idea, but my kids never forgot it. So, having a lot of ideas running around in my head has been a challenge, I need to manage them, weigh them out and if they resonate with me, I need to be careful who I tell, some people are quick to point out all the reasons why it's not a good idea.

I'm also a starter, some of those ideas get off the ground, and I know from experience that I need to be on the lookout for my replacement to run the thing because very soon I will get a new idea and be off on a new adventure, in a new direction. That's been hard to understand in myself because it looks like a flaky thing to do. But I've learned there are pioneers and there are settlers and we can't all be the starter people. Some people can only get on board with things already going on.

Timothy 4:12 tells us not to let anyone think little of you because you are young. I would replace young with your individual gifts. Mine would be, don't let anyone think little of you because you start things and then leave them, or because they view your administrative gift as bossiness. There will always be those who look down on us because we aren't like them. And sometimes we are our own worst enemy. We need to begin to be aware of the gifts God has given us, especially when those things don't look like gifts to others.

> *We have different gifts according to the grace given us. If one's gift is prophecy, let him use it in proportion to his faith; if it is serving, let him serve; if it is teaching, let him teach; if it is encouraging, let him encourage; if it is giving, let him give generously; if it is leading, let him lead with diligence; if it is showing mercy, let him do it cheerfully. (Romans 12:6-8, BSB)*

We haven't all been given the same gifts. Ask God to show you what He put inside of you specifically. What are your spiritual gifts? If you're not sure there are many personality tests online that you can take. I think the more we know ourselves, the more we understand who we were created to be, and the more we can love others AS we love ourselves.

**FORGIVE:** *God, I choose to forgive* _____ *for not valuing my gifts.*

**REWIND:** *I reject the lie that my gifts should be suppressed because others don't understand them.*

**REST:** *I know the truth is that You will show me the proper way to use the gifts you have given me.*

**RESPOND:** What gifts do you feel like God has given you? _____

_____

_____

How have those gifts been misperceived by others? _____

_____

_____

_____

_____

What are the positive aspects of those gifts? _____

_____

_____

_____

_____

Look in the mirror, say, *"thank you God for me, for who you made me to be, for all the good things that you put inside me, for all the good things that I have yet to discover. Thank you that I get to reflect you."*

# Day #14 The *"I Have to Hide Who I Am"* Lie
## By Chris Glatzel

There is a disorder called social anxiety, described as the fear of being judged or under a severe amount of scrutiny. I would contend that most cases of social anxiety are directly related to a lot of the lies we have brought up in this book. I know people who are afraid of being judged for a variety of reasons, they're afraid of letting people see the real them.

Recently on Americas Got Talent a woman came out and blew everyone away with her singing. She was powerful, and amazing, but she was also overweight and somewhere in her past she had been rejected because of her size. She had a great talent, but the rejection she felt caused her to hide it away. Many of us are like that. We fear opening up and showing people the real us.

I love the song, "This is Me", from the movie, The Greatest Showman about the great circus entrepreneur, PT Barnum and the people involved in his sideshow attractions, often thought of as 'freaks'. The words powerfully address this idea of hiding ourselves away due to fearing what others will think.

*I am not a stranger to the dark*
*Hide away, they say*
*'Cause we don't want your broken parts*
*I've learned to be ashamed of all my scars*
*Run away, they say*
*No one'll love you as you are*
*But I won't let them break me down to dust*
*I know that there's a place for us*
*For we are glorious*

*When the sharpest words wanna cut me down*

*I'm gonna send a flood, gonna drown them out*

*I am brave, I am bruised*

*I am who I'm meant to be, this is me*

*Look out 'cause here I come*

*And I'm marching on to the beat I drum*

*I'm not scared to be seen*

*I make no apologies, this is me*

*Oh-oh-oh-oh*

*Oh-oh-oh-oh*

*Oh-oh-oh-oh*

*Oh-oh-oh-oh*

*Oh-oh-oh, oh-oh-oh, oh-oh-oh, oh, oh*

*Another round of bullets hits my skin*

*Well, fire away 'cause today, I won't let the shame sink in*

*We are...*

The whole movie, in fact, speaks to coming out of our darkness and being who we really are. It's not just what we do, it really comes down to who we are. In our core. Shame keeps us hidden and tells us we will be mocked and judged if people see the real us. The best way to find out who we really are is to ask God to show us.

For many of us, we are confused about our true identities, we are presenting a façade to others that isn't really us. Similar to the lie we addressed on day 13, for example, if I think I am bossy, I hide my administrative personality. But in reality, I was meant to lead the way, and when I accept that, others will too.

This lie is rooted in the concern of what others think of us, but God says He already knows us inside and out, that nothing is hidden from Him, and that we need to be only concerned about what He thinks of us. No one else.

*For the word of God is alive and powerful. It is sharper than the sharpest two-edged sword, cutting between soul and spirit, between joint and marrow. It exposes our innermost thoughts and desires. Nothing in all creation is hidden from God. Everything is naked and exposed before his eyes, and he is the one to whom we are accountable. (Hebrews 4:12-13, NLT)*

Why do we feel like we have to pretend to be something we're not while hiding our true selves? Those feelings are usually attached to shame. When you felt shamed, you felt like you were bad, rather than your actions were inappropriate. Someone likely made you feel shame for expression yourself in a way they deemed inappropriate. Ask Father God when you first started agreeing with the lie that you can't express your true self, that you need to hide it away, because if people really knew you they wouldn't like you.

The Bible also says in James 2:8 that you are to love your neighbor AS yourself. It's even called the royal law, or as we would say 'the golden rule'. As yourself means, 'in the same way as' and we all agree that we need to love our neighbor. But we can only really love others when we begin to love ourselves. Start by asking Father God what He likes about you. And then agree with him.

**FORGIVE:** *God, I choose to forgive _____ for shaming me and making me feel like I couldn't show others my true self.*

**REWIND:** *I reject the lie that who You have created me to be is bad in any way.*

**REST:** *I know the truth is that You have created me uniquely and that I* *can be bold and confident in who I am.*

**RESPOND:** What aspects of yourself have you felt that you need to hide away? _____

_____

_____

_____

What steps could you take to help you show those parts of yourself to others?

_____

_____

_____

_____

_____

## Day #15 The "*My Feelings Aren't Valid*" Lie
### By Chris Glatzel

For anyone who second guesses themselves or has to work themselves up into a frenzy just to express themselves this is for you. What is the lie that has caused you to believe that your opinions are not valid? That you aren't important enough to say anything unless you are really upset.

I've noticed this trait in a few people around me. They seem to think that what they say has no value. They essentially have lost their voice. They have a hard time speaking up at work, or in a group, feeling that what they say is dumb or not relevant. They may make a decision and then drive themselves and others crazy for weeks afterwards wondering if it was the right decision. Or they take forever to land on a decision because they worry that it's the wrong one. They constantly fear that they will be wrong or perceived as wrong. The lie is that their thoughts and opinions aren't valid.

This lie leads you to believe you have no say. For example, I have a friend who was married for 30 years, then one day she left. Afterwards it came out that she had doubts from the beginning, but that she was afraid to say something. She felt she was doing the "right" thing according to what she perceived the people around her thought. Even if she had the nerve to speak up, and find her voice, the people around her might have talked her out of it.

As a result, many years later, she was still looking for 'happiness'. She had lived her entire life according to someone else's expectations of her and for some reason, picked that moment to break out and do what she thought was best for herself. Except it wasn't. She was leaving broken hearts in her wake. My question was what prevented her from coming to that conclusion so many years ago?

In retrospect her marriage might have worked, but resentment had grown into full blown despising. If she had taken responsibility for making a decision, even if it was acknowledging the mistake and getting out, or for dealing with the built-up resentment, perhaps she could have forgiven her husband, learned to love herself and become a happy, loving part of good relationship. Instead, because she never created good boundaries for herself and allowed her decision making to be influenced by what she thought others would think, she didn't make a decision until she got to a point of no-return and simply walked away.

We need to allow ourselves to have real feelings, good or bad. And trust the Holy Spirit to guide us instead of living by the expectations from people outside of us. When we allow others to be pulled this way and that way by the expectations of others we are like the double-minded man the Bible speaks of.

*He who doubts is like a wave of the sea, blown and tossed by the wind. That man should not expect to receive anything from the Lord. He is a double-minded man, unstable in all his ways. (James 1:6b-8. BSB)*

The opposite of being a double-minded man (or woman) is to follow the instructions in verses 5-6a.

*If any of you lacks wisdom, he should ask God, who gives generously to all without finding fault, and it will be given to him. But let him ask in faith without doubting. (BSB)*

You have to make decisions. And sometimes those decisions come with risks. It is possible that you'll make the wrong one, but not making any decision is worse. In fact, I've heard it said that not making a decision is in itself a decision. You are deciding not to do anything.

As you learn to listen to the Holy Spirit's guidance you will walk in more and more confidence. A good rule to go by is to ask for wisdom, not move until you feel some direction and then walk confidently in that direction until you feel a check by the Holy Spirit.

Feeling like your feelings aren't valid and that you don't have a say started somewhere in your childhood. Ask God to show you where that first started. What did He show you? _____

_____

_____

_____

Now let's process that.

**FORGIVE:** *God, I choose to forgive* _____
*For making me feel like my feelings weren't valid and that I had no ability to speak up for myself.*

**REWIND:** *I reject the lie I can't make a decision or speak my mind.*

**REST:** *I know the truth is that as I ask you for wisdom that you will guide me by your Holy Spirit.*

**RESPOND:** Identify an area that you have had difficulty making a decision in: _____

Ask the Holy Spirit for guidance and write what you feel he tells you _____

_____

_____

_____

_____

# Day #16 The *"I'm Too Sensitive"* Lie
## By Sharon Letson

Have you ever been told you are *too* sensitive? I have. And I hated it. I usually didn't react well. Eventually I began to think of snappy comebacks like, "Who are you that you get to determine how sensitive I should or shouldn't be?" or "Maybe I'm not too sensitive. You're just too insensitive." Note to friends of those with sensitive natures. Criticizing them for being sensitive is never a wise move.

Haha. I really was overly sensitive. But the reality was the problem was not my sensitive nature, which is a part of the way God created me, but my *wounded* sensitive nature.

I grew up in a large family without a lot of supervision, as we've already mentioned, and there was a lot of wrestling and tussling, as well as maybe a few pokes and slugs. When you get hit once on your arm it hurts, but if you get slugged over and over again in the same spot it gets bruised and tender to the touch. I believe that's a good illustration of what happened to my sensitive nature. I received a lot of emotional hits growing up and was so wounded that even innocent comments made me very defensive.

There are a lot of great things about being a sensitive person. Sensitive people have empathy. They are compassionate and concerned for others. But when their sensitive natures get wounded, even harmless comments can inflict pain.

Another word for sensitivity is tenderheartedness. And there are a lot of places where the Bible mentions the virtues of tenderheartedness.

> *Get rid of all bitterness, rage, anger, harsh words, and slander, as well as all types of evil behavior. Instead, be kind to each other,*

> *tenderhearted, forgiving one another, just as God through Christ has forgiven you. (Ephesians 4:31-32, NLT)*

The original word for tenderhearted can also be translated as merciful and compassionate and is also found in I Peter 3:8.

> *Finally, all of you should be of one mind. Sympathize with each other. Love each other as brothers and sisters. Be tenderhearted, and keep a humble attitude. (NLT)*

We're all created with personality traits, but when those parts of us get wounded we overreact. Maybe your issue isn't oversensitivity, maybe your hurt has manifested itself as anger. In either case you are reacting to your wounds rather than the situation presenting itself. It's time to dig down to see where it all started.

What personality trait of yours do you feel got wounded in childhood?

_____

_____

How has that caused you to overreact? _____

_____

_____

_____

_____

What is the positive side of that personality trait? _____

_____

_____

_____

**FORGIVE:** *God, I choose to forgive _____ for making me feel like those parts of my personality were bad.*

**REWIND:** *I reject the lie that the nature you created me with is bad in any way.*

**REST:** *I know the truth is that there are many positive ways I can impact the world because I am _____.*

**RESPOND:** Choose something (like flowers) to represent your personality traits. Create a bouquet or create a piece of artwork like a collage or painting that represents the different aspects of your personality. Write about the experience here: _____

_____
_____
_____
_____
_____
_____
_____
_____
_____
_____
_____

# Day #17 – The *"I'm Not Worth Loving"* Lie
## by Sharon Letson

This is one of the first ways we disqualify ourselves from God's love. We have bought the lie that He can't have meant that He loves *me*, because I'm not worth loving. This lie springs from a lot of places. It could come from a feeling that you've done too many awful sinful things to be worthy of God's love or it could be from a general sense of low self-worth. Were you given a message that instilled in you a feeling of worthlessness? If so this one may be hard to root out. Remember to go over these as often as necessary. You're plowing up ground made hard by years of protecting your heart.

Think about the kind of people Jesus hung around. The woman at the well had been with five different men, none of whom were her husband. The woman caught in adultery, who some say was Mary Magdalene, the same woman who was so grateful for his compassion that she wetted his feet with her tears and dried them with her hair. Tax collectors were hated by their Jewish neighbors because they taxed them more, so they could keep some before turning the rest over to the Romans. And these are the people Jesus sought out and transformed just by being in the sphere of His love.

Jesus saw value in people that the powerful and religious had deemed undesirable. And when the Pharisees confronted him about associating with 'sinners', he told them three stories (Luke 15). Each story illustrated the extravagant love of the Father for those deemed unworthy.

The first story was about a lost sheep, who had wandered away from the flock. People can be like that too. The didn't mean to leave the safety of the shepherd, but their attention was drawn to something tantalizing just out of reach, and when they reached that something, they saw another something just a little further away. And as they continued chasing those tantalizing somethings, they unwittingly wandered further from the safety of the flock and the shepherd's watchful eye.

The poor sheep from this story may have realized at some point, that it was lost and began baaing for his companions, but he didn't know how to find them again. Instead, it was the shepherd who searched high and low looking for the one who had wandered away and rejoiced when it was found. The sheep had value to its owner, just like those sinners had value to God, and He is searching for them as diligently as the shepherd from the story searched for his sheep.

The next story features a coin. Quite an interesting choice. As an inanimate object, a coin neither loses itself nor realizes it is lost. Perhaps the group of people represented here could be classified as those that don't know themselves. They are unaware of who they belong to and have no sense of their own value. Somehow, they have slipped through the cracks of life and been lost. But the value of a coin isn't diminished just because it is lost. No matter how damaged or marred that coin is, it still holds its value, but that value cannot be utilized until it is found. Its owner knows its value and undertakes a diligent search of the house. She ultimately finds the coin and rejoices because something that was valuable was restored.

Do you identify more with the sheep who wandered away or with the coin who fell through the cracks? Why? _____

_____

_____

_____

**FORGIVE:** *God, I choose to forgive myself for my past mistakes of*

_____

_____

**REWIND:** *I reject the lie that my past mistakes define who I am. I reject the messages of unworthiness.*

**REST:** *I accept the truth that you see me as valuable and worth searching for.*

**RESPOND:** Ask God to show you how He searched for you and found you.

_____
_____
_____
_____
_____
_____
_____
_____
_____
_____
_____
_____
_____

# Day #18 – The *"I've Wandered Too Far"* Lie
## by Sharon Letson

The last story in the trio of parables of lost souls in Luke 15 is the most well-known. It is the story of a son who intentionally loses himself. He does not wander away bit by bit, he has not fallen through the cracks. Instead he insults his father by asking for his inheritance and leaves not only his home, but after selling what his father gave him, he leaves even the safety of his community to go to a faraway land. He knows the consequences of his choices will be a complete estrangement from his father. He has given up all rights to sonship that he had.

Maybe in that far away land he'll find what he's looking for, he thinks. And for a while anyway, he does. He has a great time. He is free to do whatever he wants to do, away from any restrictions on his behavior his father had placed on him.

But it doesn't last. It never does. Because that kind of freedom comes with a price. It may have felt like he had unlimited resources when he left his community with all those coins in his pocket, but because he was unwise with what he had and neither earned more, nor invested his money, he eventually ran out. He was one of those 'eat, drink and be merry for tomorrow we may die' kind of people. Only tomorrow came and he found himself without friends, resources, community, or family. And he knows the whole thing is his own fault.

The father in this third story is not like the shepherd searching for the lost sheep, or the woman searching for her missing coin, instead he waits. There is something profound in that waiting. He is so anxious for his son's return that he watches the road constantly, but he does not venture to that far country to retrieve his son. He knows his son must first realize his lostness and that when he does he will remember the home he had with his father and wander back of his own accord.

The return of a lost son is even more joyous than the finding of a lost sheep, or a missing coin. The son who had thought to fix his own dilemma by hiring himself as a servant is immediately restored as a son. The moment the father sees him on the road, he runs to intercept him before he reaches the village where he will surely be scorned for his prior insults to the father. The family ring is placed on his finger, sandals brought for his feet and the best robe given to him to wear. There was no time for penance, no judgement given. The father didn't even wait until the son delivered his prepared speech.

But there is another son in this story. One who was not lost because he chose to leave his father's home, but because even though he had all the privileges of living in his father's home, he saw the father as a taskmaster, and his obligations as a son just to complete the duties his father asked of him. He lived according to the rules, but without the relationship.

This son was unhappy when someone who had value to the Father was 'found', he complained about the extravagant celebration and refused to rejoice. But even this religious son has value to the father, who reassured him of his sonship and pleaded with him to come in to the celebration.

The father throughout this story displays a love that costs him dearly. He endures the insults of both his sons and the emotional pain their actions cause him - one who by asking for his inheritance when his father is young and healthy, has as much declared that he wished him dead, and taking a good portion of the living that was meant to sustain the family; the other by his refusal to rejoice with the father when he was celebrating the restoration of his brother. That costly love was on display again when the father runs to greet the returning son and his prompt restoration of sonship before any penance could be given.

The community would not be waiting ready to receive the returning prodigal as the father was. There would be no warm welcome from them. Instead they already considered him cut off and had he reached the edge of the village before the father intercepted him, they surely would have acted on those firmly held beliefs.

This story was told to show the Pharisees the true worth of the 'sinners' they accused Jesus of dining with and to demonstrate the very extravagant love of our Father God. Their attitude was clearly mirrored in the actions of the older son, but even this son was assured of his place in the family by the father.

Do you see yourself more as the younger son who lost himself by walking away from his father or as the older son who mistakenly believed following a set of rules was the same as relationship and judged his 'sinner' brother harshly? Why? _____

_____

**FORGIVE:** *Father God, I choose to forgive myself for* _____

_____

**REWIND:** *I reject the lie that I have walked too far away from You or that rules can be substituted for relationship.*

**REST:** *I accept the truth that you are ready and waiting for me to return home to You.*

**RESPOND:** What makes you feel close to God? Where do you connect with Him the most? Be careful not to choose something that will get you back into performance. The idea is to connect with God. If you are unsure think about taking a walk in the woods or listening to worship music. Once you hit on an idea, make an effort to spend time doing that for a short period of time each day.

What will you try? _____

How many minutes each day can you commit to that? _____

After you tried it the first time, record your impressions here. _____

_____
_____
_____
_____
_____
_____
_____
_____

# Day #19 – The *"I Am Insignificant"* Lie
## by Chris Glatzel

This lie looks similar to the "I'm not worth loving lie". It tells us that we are not like that sheep, coin, or son. We are somehow different. Obviously, those things have value, but somehow that can't apply to me. I don't know why but I often excuse myself out of all kinds of situations. I am an introvert. I know people don't suspect that about me but when I have something I am trying to sell or promote I have no problem talking to people. That's because the agenda is the important thing, not me. But when I'm given a choice to show up, wherever that may be, I struggle to even interact with others.

Thoughts go through my mind, like "I won't be missed", " I don't have anything to contribute", "Other people are more naturally friendly than I am", etc. Recently I saw all that as lies. I know it should have occurred to me a lot earlier, but the random raging thoughts are sometimes so familiar it's hard to recognize them as lies. I would think, 'why should I go to that event (party, funeral, wedding, church group, Bible study, book club, etc.) when no one will notice if I'm not there?'

"Wow where did that come from?" I wondered as I was trying to process why I felt that way. I had a significant role in my family growing up, because I was the oldest. I watched the rest of the kids often, when my mom went out, shopping or wherever. I'm not sure why but I always felt the need to organize the whole bunch to clean the house. I thought if everyone would do a little a lot would get done. Even as a 10 year-old I knew that. But the others didn't see it that way and I would get a lot of flak from them for suggesting that we all did a chore that the adults hadn't assigned.

I have often been accused by them of being bossy. But I didn't feel like I was trying to be bossy, it was just my administrative skills coming out. But the message I internalized from that was that I wasn't valued for my ideas, and there wasn't any camaraderie surrounding my vision of surprising mom with a clean house.

So maybe that's why I feel my contributions now aren't valued, or that I'm better off not making a suggestion. But God has gifted me with certain talents, just like he has gifted you, and in my brain, I'm always seeing how things could be organized to get a better result.

Remember hurricane Katrina and the people living in the Houston Astrodome? I wondered at times what I would have done if I had been there. I think I would have self-appointed myself in charge of telling people what to do about bathroom areas, and food distribution etc. I know, who thinks that way? I do.

So, I have huge ideas about how to change the world, but at the same time I don't like showing up at small gatherings. That voice in my head tells me that I have nothing to offer so why go, or that I would not be missed. What is the lie? Maybe that my ideas aren't valuable thus I'm not valuable? Perhaps being part of a big family, like I was, it felt like I could easily be replaced. Or that I was simply one of the kids, not valued as an individual. It may have felt that way to 5 or 10 year-old me, but I have carried that lie into adulthood.

In Matthew 6 Jesus speaks about insignificance. He mentions a couple of insignificant things – birds and lilies. Both of these things are common and abundant, but he makes a point of saying that God cares for each of these and provides food for the birds and beauty for the lilies.

*Look at the birds. They don't plant or harvest or store food in barns, for your heavenly Father feeds them. And aren't you far more valuable to him than they are? Can all your worries add a single moment to your life? And why worry about your clothing? Look at the lilies of the fields and how they grow. They don't work or make their clothing, yet Solomon in all his glory was not dressed as beautifully as they are. And if God cares so wonderfully for wildflowers that are here today and thrown into the fire tomorrow, he will certainly care for you. Why do you have so little faith? (vs. 26-30, NLT)*

The theme of the passage is 'don't worry', but it is part of a larger set of sermons taught by Jesus to a crowd of people while on the mountainside commonly called "The Sermon on the Mount", which begins in Chapter 5 and goes through Chapter 7.

In this passage Jesus is illustrating again the value of each of us. Focus on the parts of these verses where he declares how valuable *you* are. In verse 26 you'll find it in the question, *"And aren't you far more valuable to him than they are?"* and in verse 30 where he states, *"And if God cares so wonderfully for wildflowers that are here today and thrown into the fire tomorrow, he will certainly care for you."* Remember this when you begin to feel that you are insignificant and have nothing to offer.

What childhood experiences gave you the message that you were insignificant? _____

_____

Who made you feel insignificant? _____

**FORGIVE:** *Father, I choose to forgive* _____
*for making me feel insignificant.*

**REWIND:** *I reject the lie that you see me as insignificant.*

**REST:** *I embrace the truth that I am more precious to you than the birds you provide for and the lilies that you adorn the fields with.*

**RESPOND:** God has made you unique. Journal about all the positive traits you have: _____

_____

_____

_____

_____

Art prompt: This is similar to the vision boards you have seen people do but I'm calling it an identity board. Spend some time looking through old magazines and papers, or even on the web, you can print out a picture, and collect things that interest you, stuff you like, and images that attract you.

Once you've collected your images, begin to paste them onto a background. The order doesn't matter. Just arrange it in a way that makes you happy. The background can be a piece of card stock, construction paper or something similar. When you are done, take a look at the unique stuff you've placed on your board.

If we all did this together with the same resources, each of ours would still look vastly different, because the colors and images that attract us are different. In that fact alone, we are significant. We alone carry our outlook, wants, desires, interests and our perspective of the world around us. No one sees it just like you do. So, appreciate how you've been designed, and allow the creator to flow through your expression to others.

# Day #20 - The Lie of Recognition vs. (In)Significance
## By Sharon L Letson

I'm sure my early experiences as one of the youngest children in a large household contributed to my feelings of insignificance. Our house was a bit chaotic with all those people and it was easy to go unnoticed. Besides our parents weren't the greatest at being present in our lives. Our mom had her own emotional issues, our dad worked a lot and seemed angry all the time when he was there, and they fought – a lot. Going unnoticed was the safest course of action, but many of our emotional needs went unfulfilled.

Early abandonment and neglect issues exacerbate feelings of insignificance. But everyone longs to belong. You need to know that you matter and that your presence adds something. Someone needs what you bring to the situation. However, in longing for significance I have realized that I have unconsciously looked for recognition.

Recognition shows up when I quietly desire to be called out for my skills and talents, but it isn't a good thing. For example, I have a good singing voice. It was probably all those years of Christian school choir training that molded that, but I seem to have a need to be noticed for the way I sing. It is not something I consciously seek, but these thoughts intrude themselves. Thoughts like, "if the right person hears me sing, then they will ask me to be on the worship team". It feels good to be complimented, but because of my desire to be recognized I have had to fight the urge to sing just to be heard, rather than to sing to worship God.

I fight the same battle on many fronts. If I write a book or a blog I start to dream about when people in my life will notice and say something. It feels good imagining what they will say, but even when the compliments do come, the reality of being recognized is very different than the expectations and really doesn't satiate my craving for recognition. Any feeling they bring is fleeting and I continue to long for the next compliment. It's a crazy cycle and I'm desperately trying to hop off of the hamster wheel it keeps me on.

The early emotional neglect in my life left my starving for attention and I have sought recognition as a way to validate myself. It's as if I don't know my own worth unless someone else validates me. But God created me with worth and value and I should need to look no further than what He says about me to be grounded in my worth.

The lie here is that if I am not recognized that I am not significant. It is one way that I still operate as an orphan even though I have been adopted as a daughter of God. Sometimes it feels like I've been passed over; sometimes it feels like no one notices me, my skills, or my contributions; sometimes it is just a whisper of my heart that cries, 'notice me'.

I've realized that this is a false dichotomy. Recognition does not equal significance. It is actually a false sense of significance. It does not last, and so I find myself looking for that next moment of recognition. Even more importantly, not being recognized does not mean that I am insignificant. I have worth and value not only because God has given me gifts that can be used to build up the body of Christ, but also simply because I am His child. He delights in me and He is delighted by me. I simply have to remind myself of that.

Even though the following verses are talking about the city of Jerusalem, I don't mind appropriating them and applying them to myself because I know that in the New Testament I, as part of the church, am called the 'bride of Christ'.

*"Never again will you be called 'The Forsaken City', or 'The Desolate Land.' Your new name will be 'The City of God's Delight' and 'The Bride of God,' for the LORD delights in you and will claim you as his bride." (Isaiah 62:4-5, NLT)*

You need a new name. The old titles of broken, wounded, and suffering need to be replaced. You are the Lord's beloved and you need to begin to claim that.

**FORGIVE:** *God I choose to forgive* _____ *who neglected my emotional needs and caused a sense of lack in me.*

**REWIND:** *I reject the lie that says I have no significance unless I am validated by others. I reject recognition as a false sense of significance.*

**REST:** *I embrace the truth that I am loved and beloved by you. That I am significant because You claim me as Your own and because You have given me gifts and talents that I should be using to bless others with.*

**RESPOND:** Do you find yourself seeking recognition as a way to feel significant like I have? What do you want to be recognized for? _____
_____
_____

How do you respond to compliments? _____
_____
_____

Does receiving compliments satisfy your longing for recognition? _____
_____

How can you adjust your thinking so that you are getting your validation from who God says you are and not from others recognizing your talents? _____

# Day #21 – The *"I Am Invisible"* Lie
## by Chris Glatzel

Another aspect of this lie of insignificance is a feeling of being invisible. The lie of invisibility says that even if I'm there, no one will notice. When I realized I was believing this lie, I asked God where it first started. In my memory I went back to grade school, where I often felt like I wanted to shrink into the wallpaper. We were a big family of 7 kids born within 10 years. We were poor and didn't have much to be proud of at home. Our house was always a mess, and I was embarrassed to bring friends home. Our parents were super young when they had me. They got married within a few weeks of turning 17 and 19. They were kids, having kids!

I am a mom of 6 myself and even though they were more spaced out, it was still a difficult thing to keep the house all together when they were growing up, so I can't blame my mom. So, as an adult I understand how that can be an overwhelming job, but when you are a kid living it, you believe what your environment tells you. For me it was that there was no intention by my parents to have me, so how could God have intention for my life. There was no value in my presence, we weren't important, and we needed to stay in the shadows.

This lie feeds the idea that I don't matter to others. Even when I do go places, I'm not there. Instead, I spend a lot of time in my head. I can be planning my lunch or what I'm going to do tomorrow etc. I realize that I don't remember a lot of my childhood because I probably wasn't living it. I was in another world. They say that your mind is like a bad neighborhood. You don't want to go there alone, but that's where I seem to spend most of my time.

When you don't think that you are significant in any way, you aren't thinking that the people you are with need any input from you. Sometimes when I am at church groups or with friends, I'm focused on what I might be getting out of the interactions, instead of asking what I can give to the others I'm with. As the body of Christ, that's a bit like being the broken or gashed appendage that needs all the attention the body can muster, or like being the arm that's cut off, and trying to survive on its own. It's not contributing or taking. It's just withering away by itself.

I Corinthians 12:12 says:

> *"The human body has many parts, but the many parts make up one whole body. So it is with the body of Christ." (NLT)*

You may think you are only the pinky toe of the body of Christ, but no part is invaluable. Have you ever tried to walk when your pinky toe was hurting? Can you imagine trying to walk without one? The body of Christ needs you to be a vibrant, healthy, and contributing part.

I have to constantly battle the thoughts that tell me, *"I don't want to go, no one will miss me if I don't go, or notice me if I am there".* Then if I do decide I need to go, especially if I'm the one in charge, (I get myself into situations like this, because of those aforementioned administrative skills) I battle the thoughts, *"what's here for me?"* I don't see myself as the major contributor, but the one that needs the most help.

But if our example is supposed to be Jesus, we see that His heart comes into the room to see the needs of others and pours the resources of heaven into them. What a huge lie we are all believing if we buy into the thought that we have nothing to give. We all have something to offer. So why the battle?

I'm sure it's different for everyone, and I've tried to sort out where mine came from. I believe I got some insight recently when I decided to attend a workshop. I was tired, and my thoughts were "oh good, I need a refreshing", but on the lengthy drive there, God gently started to invade my mental meanderings, nudging me that maybe there would be someone there that He could speak to through me. And reminding me that I have a lot of wisdom that He has given me over the years to share, maybe there is someone who needs to hear that. At the conference there were strong leaders that were highly organized, so my administration skills didn't need to kick in. I felt like a beginner, but I cooperated and contributed, and it was good.

God and I are still working on this thing. Can I look in the mirror and say I am significant? When I walk into the room do I bring a presence of (His) greatness? It's like the scripture about hiding your light under a bushel. First, we have to believe that we have a light.

What childhood experiences gave you the message that you were invisible?
_____

Who made you feel this way? _____.

Ask God to show you where He was at that moment. Record that here: _____
_____
_____

**FORGIVE:** *Father, I choose to forgive* _____
*for making me feel invisible.*

**REWIND:** *I reject the lie that you see me as insignificant.*

**REST:** *I embrace the truth that I am a valuable part of the body, that I carry the light and presence of who You are to the world.*

**RESPOND:** What part of the "body" do you feel like? What makes that part valuable? What would happen to the body without it? _____

_____
_____
_____
_____
_____
_____

# Day #22 – The "*Invisible is Safer*" Lie
## by Sharon Letson

In some cases, invisibility actually feels like a safer option than being open, honest and vulnerable. Vulnerability gets you hurt. There have been too many people who have contributed to the damage in your heart and therefore you retreat from human interaction. You have built an impenetrable wall around your heart and have no plans to let anyone past it.

Retreating as a way of coping with the scariness of life started early for me. Being one of the younger children in a large family contributed to the feelings of invisibility, as we were never singled out for anything positive. I was just one of the bunch. And our dad had a horrible habit of calling us every name but our own. He was also a big scary guy, who worked too much and never really wanted so many kids. When he did come home, staying out of the way was better than getting yelled at or worse.

Hiding felt calming and comforting to me. I could fit into the smallest spaces and I would just stay there. One of my favorites was behind the piano. It had been pushed up against an unused door and the doorway provided just enough space for me to sit in once I squeezed behind the piano.

Later in my life a therapist called it my "flight or fight" instinct. When life felt threatening, I chose flight every time. Even as an adult, it did not feel safe to me to open up to people. I felt if they really knew who I was inside that they would reject me or judge me. This is in opposition to the other side of feeling invisible that cries to be known, to be recognized and valued. This side likes being ignored. I was the one who walked into church and preferred being able to slip into the pew, absorb what I could from the service and slip out again before being cornered by someone who wanted to shake my hand, speak to me, or God forbid, try to hug me. For me, church greeting time was tortuous.

Naturally you have likely been in many situations that did not feel safe and there are people who do not deserve your trust. As mentioned before, some of your reactions are valid responses that were necessary to keep you safe. In fact, your heart may have become so wounded that it is very bruised and even the slightest touch inflicts fresh pain. But what usually happens is that you now have a conditioned response that is being applied mistakenly to new situations. It is unlikely that the good folks at the corner church are intent on emotionally wounding you.

If you find yourself overreacting to situations in this manner, retreating rather than interacting, even though it may be rooted in a very valid place, it is still a lie that needs to be addressed.

The first step in addressing this lie is learning to establish appropriate boundaries in your relationships. If you seem to always allow people in your life who take advantage of you and who constantly seem to be crossing lines into areas that make you feel uncomfortable, you may have a boundary issue.

Or maybe you are the one who overshares with people who have not yet earned a place of trust in your life. For learning how to establish good boundaries, we recommend the book, <u>Boundaries: When to Say Yes, How to Say No to Take Control of Your Life</u> by Henry Cloud and John Townsend.

Once you feel confident that you have the knowledge you need to establish appropriate boundaries with people, you will hopefully feel a little more confident interacting with them. But if that's not the case we need to look at what retreating from even casual relationships is costing you, and them.

You see, you are looking at the situation only from the point of view of protecting your heart and keeping yourself safe. The lie is that protecting your heart is necessary and more important than what you have to offer to others, the skills you have to contribute, or what your care and concern would mean to them. It also is a mistaken belief that if you are more open with people that you will continue to be hurt by them, judged or criticized.

Your heart needs to heal and that takes time, but as it does you need to begin stepping out and interacting in small ways. Try a smile, a handshake and when you're ready, let that one woman who just has to hug everyone, give you a squeeze. We are not meant to live in isolation. And it isn't emotionally healthy to be so inwardly focused.

Many people long to be loved, but are so afraid they'll get hurt that they cut themselves off from others. They've been so conditioned to retreat that they don't really know healthy ways of interacting. I was one of those, always wrapped up in my own hurts to the point that I was not showing concern to others.

> I Thessalonians 4:9 & 10 tells us, *"But we don't' need to write to you about the importance of loving each other, for God himself has taught you to love one another. Indeed, you already show your love for all the believers, throughout Macedonia. Even so, dear brothers and sisters, we urge you to love them even more." (NLT)*

Obviously loving each other is an important quality among Christians and you have as much responsibility to show the love of God to others as they have to show it to you. The more you focus on your own woundedness the less you have to give to others. It isn't always about you and your wounded heart. Other people have hurts and issues as well. Begin to think about how you can help and support others. Not to the point of not having anything left to care for yourself, but enough to begin having meaningful relationships.

**FORGIVE:** *Father I choose to forgive those that have hurt me and myself for being self-focused and not seeing the needs of others.*

**REWIND:** *I reject the lie that my woundedness is beyond the reach of Your love to heal. I invite You into my situations and hurts to begin healing my wounded heart. Thank you that you'll help me look beyond my own hurts and truly see the people around me.*

**REST:** *I embrace the truth that not only do I have something to offer them, that I have a responsibility as a Christian to show love to others.*

**RESPOND:** Think about another person you know with hurts and issues of their own. How could you show the love of Jesus to them? Think about writing them a note of encouragement, a phone call to ask how they are, or meeting them for a cup of coffee. Remember this is time to focus on them, not on yourself. Record your interaction here: _____

_____
_____
_____
_____
_____
_____
_____
_____
_____

# Day #23 – The *"I Am Unwanted"* Lie
## by Sharon Letson

This lie comes from early messages of abandonment and neglect. When you spend your life without a consistent message of being wanted and cared for, you end up being the one who has to look out for your own best interests. You have learned to be strong, because you've had to be, but you've always longed for someone you could rely on to be strong with you or for you.

I learned early on that our dad didn't want seven kids. I often heard him mention that he only wanted four. As one of the youngest three it never felt good to hear that. In addition, he beratingly referred to us as the dingbat (our mom) and the seven little ding-dongs. Of course, I understand now that because our dad came from an even larger, more dysfunctional family then ours, that he felt overly responsible for his own younger brothers and sisters who were still growing up while he was raising his own kids and he knew the challenges a large family brought.

It was our mother who chose to continue having kids until she got what she thought was her ideal – two little girls, but she was unprepared for the reality of those seven little human beings. I was the older of those two youngest girls, soon eclipsed by the baby of the family, and totally out-maneuvered by my older brothers and the first-born, my sister Chris.

There were so many of us and we were so often spoken to as a group that our individual selves got lost. We were just one of those Whittaker kids. Not given much individual attention by our parents (at least not positive), not praised for any individual traits, and as parents of large families are wont to do – often called by the wrong name.

My father still jokingly refers to me as, "the one who insists her name is not Karen." I can laugh now, but it bothered me as a child. How could my own father not know my name? The messages we all received were that we were not special, or a positive addition to our parents' lives. We were only a bother to be dealt with and corrected.

Or consider the case of a friend of my sister's. He woke up one morning to a completely empty house. His mother had just left him there. He was only 12. From that point on he was mostly on his own with only some occasional contact with his father. Even as an adult he struggles with trust and forgiveness.

The good news is that no matter how ignored or neglected you were as a child, even if you had a parent that totally abdicated their parental responsibilities, you have a Father in Heaven who knows your name, and who planned your existence. You were not a surprise to Him, not an unwanted addition to His family.

But because you've had to do it alone it becomes hard to believe that God, who feels so removed from you, actually wants to walk with you through the difficult places in life.

There is a lot of comfort in David's psalms and Psalm 27 is no exception.

> *Hear my voice when I call, O Lord: be merciful to me and answer me. My heart says of you, "Seek his face!" Your face, Lord, I will seek. Do not hide your face from me, do not turn your servant away in anger; you have been my helper. Do not reject me or forsake me, O God my Savior. Though my father and mother forsake me, the Lord will receive me. (7-10, NIV)*

Read that last sentence again. *Though my father and mother forsake me, the Lord will receive me.* What a wonderful thought. Our earthly parents were imperfect, flawed people, raised by imperfect, flawed people and who raised us as imperfect, flawed people. Maybe in your experience they weren't involved at all. But God is always waiting for us to turn to Him. His arms are open to receive us into His embrace.

As we can see in this psalm, David got discouraged, as many of us do, but he knew where to look for comfort. We often pull back from God when we feel discouraged, but David knew what he had to do. He sought God's face and he knew he would be received. We pull back because that is what we are used to. Our experiences have taught us that no one will be there for us, but God will be when we turn to Him.

Some of David's other psalms are less fraught with internal turmoil like this one from Psalm 68.

> *Sing to God, sing praise to his name, extol him who rides on the clouds – his name is the Lord – and rejoice before him. A father to the fatherless, a defender of widows, is God in his holy dwelling. God sets the lonely in families, he leads forth the prisoners with singing. (4-6, NIV)*

God has always been a God of the downtrodden, of those that the powerful of the world find little value in. We can take comfort that no matter our family situation, we have a Father who cares and is concerned about our lives. I believe the family that God sets the lonely in is the church family. We have to allow those people in, to love us and that means being willing to be vulnerable with them. They can't get to know you if you scoot out the door before the last amen is said.

**FORGIVE:** *God, I chose to forgive my parents for neglecting my needs and leaving me to care for myself.*

**REWIND:** *I reject the lie that you will neglect or abandon me.*

**REST:** *I accept the truth that You will be a father to me, that whenever I come to You that you will be there for me and walk through life with me.*

**RESPOND:** Are you lonely, looking for a family to be a part of? The church is meant to be that family and yet it isn't always. How have you tried to connect to people around you? _____

_____

_____

How has it worked so far? _____

_____

_____

_____

_____

_____

_____

_____

_____

Remember that connecting is going to take effort on your part as well. Don't give up if it doesn't work perfectly at first. Maybe a small group, or Bible Study would be a good starting point.

## Day #24 - Comparison Leads to Jealousy
### By Chris Glatzel

Why do I feel this overwhelming feeling that, if given a choice people would choose to hang out with others over me, that they like them better? Or that I'm not a good friend? I've met them. I'm nice to them. So, why do they all hang out with someone else instead of me?

Where did I first start believing the lie that I'm not a person people would want to be friends with? Or that if others are chosen over me, that means I am less than them? When I say that out loud, it doesn't make sense, because I do have friends, and we get together and have a great time.

Or sometimes I feel left out. When groups are assigned and tasks handed out, I think, "why wasn't I included?" Or "why did that person get that job or that compliment? That's the one I wanted." Sometimes even when I hear someone pray, I feel like I should pray like that. That somehow they are better than me because of how they pray.

What's the issue? Love says I should be happy for others when they are blessed and consider others before myself. Besides, I get included when my skills are needed, but I still get this feeling when I see other people get a compliment or task I want to be considered for. Or sometimes I have a subconscious thought that gets triggered, perhaps by something innocent like by what I see on social media. I see other businesses similar to mine and have thoughts like, "I'm not doing enough. People won't want to come to me as a person or as a business. We aren't doing all the cool things they are."

Comparing myself to others leads to me feeling insecure and it opens the door for jealousy to grow in me. When this comparison/jealousy issue pops up, I ask God what the lie is that I'm believing. And He has shown me that it goes back to my childhood again, being the poor kid, with the clothes that didn't fit right, the messy house, and the government food. I didn't feel like I measured up then and it was that feeling that was still hanging around.

I have forgiven my parents. They were doing the best they could, and I forgave any classmates that might have made me feel that way. I'm sure now, that they didn't think those things, but tell that to my childhood self.

I've started being able to identify that feeling of being left out when I compare myself to someone else or feel jealous of them. It's a thought process that I have to deal with occasionally, so I have to find some truth to meditate on to combat the lies. In I Corinthians 3, I find that jealousy is part of my sinful nature which I'm trying to grow out of.

> *You are jealous of one another and quarrel with each other. Doesn't that prove you are controlled by your sinful nature? Aren't you living like people of the world? (I Corinthians 3:3, NLT)*

God is calling us to live differently than people of the world and when we are comparing ourselves to others, instead of growing more God-like we are feeding a part of us that we don't want to encourage – jealousy.

He tells us that He has plans for us. Those plans are specific to you. The plan He has for someone else is not the same plan He has for you.

> *"For I know the plans I have for you", says the Lord. "They are plans for good and not for disaster, to give you a future and a hope." (Jer. 29:11, NLT)*

So, when you begin to feel left out remind yourself to stop comparing yourself to someone else, to be happy for them, and thank God for the specific awesome plan He has in store for you.

**FORGIVE:** *God, I chose to forgive myself for allowing jealousy to grow in my heart.*

**REWIND:** *I reject the lie that when I feel left out that means I am unwanted.*

**REST:** *I accept the truth that You have something special in mind for me. That you have friends and opportunities intended just for me.*

**RESPOND:** What makes you feel jealous or left out? _____

_____
_____
_____
_____

Write out what you plan to tell yourself the next time feelings of jealousy start to well up in your heart: _____

_____
_____
_____
_____
_____
_____
_____
_____
_____
_____
_____
_____

# Day #25 – Fear of Failure
## By Chris Glatzel

Somedays I have a fear of failure. Like every decision I make is going to go wrong somehow. I try to over prepare just in case something happens, but there is always this nagging feeling that it's not going to be good enough. Can you relate? So, explore with God some reasons why you might be afraid to fail. Was there a traumatic experience related to this? A time perhaps when you thought you were prepared and it didn't turn out very well?

Back when I was in college, I joined a quartet singing group. We practiced quite a bit, but when it got to the performance I forgot my alto part and just sang the melody. It was not a complete flop, but I "failed" at pulling up my end. That left me a bit gun shy about doing that kind of thing again. I did eventually join a choir, but it took me a long time until I felt I could do the small ensemble deal.

I know this is a minor example, and I'm sure I could find a few dozen more that are buried in my bucket of embarrassing memories. I wasn't devastated or anything, but I had that, "oh crap, I totally messed up - again" feeling go through me.

Some people find those experiences debilitating. Especially if they are perfectionists, or if there is outside pressure to perform. Doing things with excellence is different than feeling the need to always be perfect. Because it's never perfect, but if you gave it your best effort and attention, you can relax and say, "I did it with excellence". That subtle shift in attitude brings freedom.

Several times over the past 20+ years my children, one at a time, have taken me aside to talk. They expressed hurt or anger. They didn't feel loved. They felt ignored or were disappointed by my actions. My oldest tended to write me letters to get his feelings out, but most of them have chosen to just be silent when they were feeling these things.

We all get hurt by those that love us most. I am pretty sure I've never been brave enough to share my true feelings with my parents. It would be to spare their feelings, so I get why some of my children haven't said anything.

So, in the past when the conversation started with, "Mom, I need to talk to you about something" with a certain tone of voice, or I would get a letter, I would get fearful. And then when the actual conversation happened I would be so buried in shame that I could barely function, let alone talk about it.

When someone is telling you that your actions hurt them, it's a hard thing to take. Feelings of remorse, anger, repentance, excuses, or rationalizations start - pick one or all, like I tend to do. I go through all the phases, and then end up feeling horrible, like there is no hope of me being a decent human, let alone a good mom. "No hope is a sign that you are believing a lie," Bill Johnson from Bethel Church in Redding, California has said.

Just recently this happened again. My sweet baby (she's 19) approached me humbly with a lump in her throat and said, "Mom, I was angry at you because I wanted to share with you about my mission's trip and all you wanted to talk about was logistics." And all of the emotions showed up in me at once.

Anger, "well how dare she, I am concerned about getting her back home". And "Oh man, I've done it again. I'm a terrible person", or "well it's my love language to organize and help". I squeaked out an "I'm sorry" and tried to think of some good questions. But this nagging thing kept coming back, telling me I was just incapable of loving. Then I didn't like myself very much. And how can I receive God's love if I feel I am unlovable? It's a vicious cycle.

After a week or so and she was back to her sweet self and I was forgiven. But as I was sitting alone with the Lord today, I was feeling kinda' depressed, and I started to look for the reason I was feeling that way. When I got to Mari is coming home, I started crying. I was believing the lie that I'm incapable of loving her well, and it was causing fear to creep in.

There is a formula that I can clearly see needs to be implemented when others have these emotions, but recognizing it in myself it becomes much less clear. When I saw that I was feeling fear about her coming home, I asked myself what the lie was that I was believing. It was that I'm a failure as a mom. Even though I had dealt with that 'thing' years ago and thought it was in the past, when I agree to lies, it's an open invitation for them to move back in.

Shame says you are a failure and there is no hope, while true conviction from God says you have failed but repent, get up and try again. I love the way you are. Because I believed the lie, I was feeling no hope, and just knew that I would fail to show her love well enough. I repented for agreeing with that lie. I repented for not loving myself. I thanked God for the way He made me, and that HE loved me like I am. I forgave myself for the times I failed. And asked Him to continue to take the failures and teach me how to love like He does. Whew. The fear lifted, and the hopelessness turned to joy. What a difference seeing the truth makes.

> *Therefore, there is now no condemnation for those who are in Christ Jesus, because through Christ Jesus the law of the Spirit who gives life has set you free from the law of sin and death. (Romans 8:1-2, NIV)*

We've already seen that the only way to keep the law completely is to have no law to keep. We are no longer living under condemnation. I have been set free from that. So why am I condemning myself if He doesn't condemn me?

There are many questions that we can ask Father God when these lies try to creep in. For example,

*Jesus, where were you when I messed up?*

*Jesus, what were you feeling?*

*Is there anyone I need to forgive for that time? (Even if its yourself)*

*What lie did I believe regarding my failure(s).*

*Jesus, what is the truth?*

**FORGIVE:** *God, I chose to forgive myself for my many failures in the area(s) of* _____

_____

_____.

**REWIND:** *I reject the lie that those past failures mean I am a failure as a person.*

**REST:** *I accept the truth that as I continue to grow in You and become more like You that I will succeed at* _____

_____

_____

**RESPOND:** Think about the main area you feel you have failed in. What would success in that area of your life look like? What would it feel like? ____

_____

_____

_____

_____

_____

## Day #26 – Shame Says You Are Bad
### By Chris Glatzel

I messed up again. Just so you know, these things happen to everyone, but what I've found, is that if we have decided to belong to God, we are immediately entered into a war. And the enemy of our souls is out to destroy us, even long before we make that decision. So, when we make a mistake he introduces a lie. That lie is that we are a mistake, or if we do something bad, we are bad. If we fail once or even a few times, we are a failure.

LIES! He's the father of lies, and the accuser. You were created in the image of the Almighty God, and it is a lie that says you are ruined, or something is wrong with you. That spirit is called shame. The difference between guilt and shame is, I've *done* something wrong vs I *am* something wrong.

If God created you in His image, then you are not something wrong. The only reason Adam was kicked out of paradise was because He believed a lie. And we have the same choice, if we believe the truth about who we are, we can be with Him in paradise today. It's kind of amazing.

So, what to do when you honestly mess up? I've seen close friends beat themselves up for days. It's like they think that if they punish themselves enough they can atone for their mistakes. But the reality is that Jesus already atoned for all of it.

So, what do we do when we honestly blew it in a big way? We confess our sins and He is faithful to forgive us. We go to those who we might have hurt, and we clean up our mess. Forgiveness is the key to so much.

When we've fallen in a huge pit, God doesn't look down and say, "well now you've done it, there's no way out of there" No! He says, "here take my hand. Let's get you up, you are too good to be down there. You belong up here." I've heard it said this way. When God shows you your mess, thank Him for redirecting you and for offering righteousness, peace, and joy.

I had coffee with a friend of mine the other day. She was having a down day. If she wrote her life story it would be hard for people to believe. But at that time, she was drowning in guilt and shame. Her husband had committed suicide and she blamed herself. She had given her children up for adoption, because when she looked at them, she would see her husband in their eyes, mannerisms, features, and she could hardly stand to be around them. This nagging little voice inside her head constantly reminded her of the trauma of the suicide, the grief she hasn't let herself feel, and the pointing fingers of shame, telling her it was all her fault.

She's a very busy person, because being at rest brings up all the thoughts of self-hatred, so she just keeps moving and trying not to think or feel. After we chatted, she realized she needed some divine assistance with this. We prayed, forgiving him for taking his life, and forgiving herself. We told condemnation and self-hatred to leave in Jesus name and she accepted the love and forgiveness of Father God.

She might have to repeat this often, because those old lies are deeply planted, but a couple days later she called me and said, "Oh man, I feel so much better, I AM forgiven! I am LOVED!"

What about you? Are there things in your life that weigh heavy on you, like you are carrying a 500 lb rock on your back? Take the time to ask Father God to take that off. Most of the time He can just lift it when you release it to Him. Through forgiveness and confessing the truth of His love for you.

In prophetically speaking of Jesus, Isaiah says:

*The Spirit of the Sovereign Lord is on me, because the Lord has anointed me to proclaim good news to the poor. He has sent me to bind up the brokenhearted, to proclaim freedom for the captives and release from darkness for the prisoners, to proclaim the year of the Lord's favor and the day of vengeance of our God, to comfort all who mourn, and provide for those who grieve in Zion – to bestow on them a crown of beauty instead of ashes, the oil of joy instead of mourning, and a garment of praise instead of a spirit of despair. (Isaiah 61:1-3, NIV)*

He's a good Father. We can come to Him with all our stuff. It's the great exchange program. Beauty for ashes, the oil of joy for mourning, laughter for the spirit of heaviness. Hallelujah! When we feel shame, we know that God is not the one condemning us.

**FORGIVE:** *God, I chose to forgive myself for* _____ *and for taking on shame.*

**REWIND:** *I reject the lie that I need to carry shame in an attempt to atone for my mistakes.*

**REST:** *I accept the truth that You have already atoned for my sins and that there is no condemnation in You.*

**RESPOND:** What has been weighing you down? _____

_____

_____

What message has the enemy been telling you to make you feel shame? _____

_____

As you give it to God what do you see Him giving you in exchange for that shame? _____

## Day #27 – The *"I Am Unqualified"* Lie
### By Chris Glatzel

I was recently visiting some friends that own a business. They had just hired an administrator and they said she was the best detailed, hard-working admin that they have ever had. The owners of the business think she is doing a great job and tell her repeatedly. But she made a couple of mistakes in the process of learning her new roles and kept asking if she's fired.

My friend said it makes sense because they know the family, and this woman has been so berated verbally, that she has come to see herself that way. Because she has agreed with the lies spoken to her for so many years, it will take an incredible amount of self-awareness, willpower, and a downright miracle for her to see herself differently. I'm hoping the positive work environment with lots of encouragement will be a start. If she doesn't sabotage the job with her poor self-image.

But the truth is when God gives us gifts and talents to use, He also gives us the grace to use them. I've heard grace described as unmerited favor, but it is more than that. If we look at the verses where grace is used along with the gifts we are given, we can see that grace is the empowerment to use that gift.

> *But he gives us even more grace to stand against such evil desires.* (James 4:6b, NLT)

Grace as used in this scripture is power. Power to do what we've been called to do. It refers to God freely extending Himself to people because He wants to be near them and bless them. God comes near to us and blesses us with the ability to do what He's gifted us to do. It is something we receive.

> *For from his fullness, we have all received grace upon grace.* (John 1:16, BSB)

It's something that we are instructed to grow in.

*But grow in the grace and knowledge of our Lord and Savior Jesus Christ. (2 Peter 3:18a, NIV)*

And it is attached to the gifts we are each given.

*We have different gifts, according to the grace given to each of us. (Romans 12:6a, NIV)*

When God gives us gifts and talents, He also gives us the grace or ability to operate in those gifts. In other words, we are already qualified because the qualifications come with the gift. It is a package deal.

*It is not that we think we are qualified to do anything on our own. Our qualification comes from God. (2 Corinthians 3:5, NLT)*

But lies, spoken often enough, look like truth, especially when they are told to our young selves. How many of us have believed the lies that we have been told over the years? Even when others tell us good things, we believe the bad instead.

Wherever your pain came from, the answer is always the same, forgiveness, and examining what the circumstances told you that was a lie. You are more than what your environment has formed you to be. You are created in HIS image, and when you get rid of the lies you've believed about Father God based on your own experiences with earthly parents, you can begin to be your real self, the way you were designed. We get to reflect the Son, like the moon reflects the sun.

Let's examine our hearts and find the lies. Ask God for the truth. Repent for believing the worst of ourselves.

**FORGIVE:** *God, I chose to forgive _____ for making me feel unqualified.*

**REWIND:** *I reject the lie that I am not qualified for the work you've given me to do.*

**REST:** *I accept the truth that You have given me the grace, or empowerment, to use the gifts that you have given me.*

**RESPOND:** List the giftings that God has given you. _____
_____
_____
_____
_____
_____

How has he qualified you to operate in those gifts? _____
_____
_____
_____
_____
_____
_____
_____
_____
_____
_____
_____
_____
_____

# Day #28 – The *"My Thoughts Condemn Me"* Lie
## By Chris Glatzel

Sometimes I have a crabby day, or a grumpy week, and my attitude is bad all around. Add to that a few people getting on my last nerve and my attitude is really in the dumpster. Recently I came to the realization that this bad attitude often starts with an attitude of judgement towards someone. Or sometimes it is a reaction to an annoyance I hadn't forgiven yet.

When my bad attitude is stinking thinking, its real easy to slip off the path to the wrong side of the road and end up in the ditch. That's when I wonder, "do the thoughts we think condemn us?"

Well, I think the answer is yes and no. It really depends on what we do with those thoughts, doesn't it? We have choices. Sometime the thoughts are gut reactions, or they come from somewhere deep in our subconscious and are triggered by skewed perceptions. Other times the thoughts are arrows like those mentioned in Ephesians, that we need our shield of faith to defend against. But sometimes our faith shields are down and, the enemy lands one in a vulnerable area.

Or perhaps the thoughts are from God. It could be that you have a high sense of discernment. So, if we handle the thoughts correctly, we can stay in right relationship with God and we are at peace. If we let the thoughts marinate and we don't address them, we have disconnection and no peace. The goal of our lives should be constant connection to Father God. If that breaks down it's a good indicator that there is some wrong thinking going on.

Handling thoughts incorrectly could look like, agreeing with them and developing a bad, ornery attitude. Or worse yet acting on them. Handling them right looks like, asking Father God a lot of questions.

If the thoughts are temptation. Stop and worship and praise him for the fact that he has freed you from all that. If its doubting God, ask Him for the truth and then praise him. If it's criticism toward another person, pray for them and bless them. Even if the thought is from God about them, the response is the same. You can slide from judgment and condemnation into blessing and intercession very easily. Maybe God is showing you something to pray about. Maybe Satan is trying to put a kink in your relationship with that person. Same response.

> *And this is my prayer: that your love may abound more and more in knowledge and depth of insight, so that you may be able to discern what is best and may be pure and blameless for the day of Christ, filled with the fruit of righteousness that comes through Jesus Christ – to the glory and praise of God. (Philippians 1:9-11, NIV)*

Discernment and judgment are two sides of the same coin. Discernment comes when we abound in love. Without love we fall into judgement. It's all in what you do with it. God wants to show us our mess, but not to condemn us. It's for the purpose of reconciliation. Same with your own hearts. He never condemns. He's more interested in showing us a better way. It's His great exchange program.

> *What then shall we say in response to these things? If God is for us, who can be against us? He who did not spare His own Son but gave Him up for us all, how will He not also, along with Him, freely give us all things? Who will bring any charge against God's elect? It is God who justifies. Who is there to condemn us? For Christ Jesus who died, and more than that was raised to life, is at the right hand of God – and He is interceding for us. (Romans 8:31-34, BSB)*

**FORGIVE:** *God, I chose to forgive myself for having unloving and judgmental thoughts. I choose to forgive those I feel have slighted me or made bad choices.*

**REWIND:** *I reject the lie that having bad or negative thoughts condemns me.*

**REST:** *I accept the truth that as I walk in Your love that I will have discernment rather than a judgmental attitude.*

**RESPOND:** Think about a person or situation that you have been judgmental toward. Write out those judgmental thoughts here: _____

_____
_____
_____
_____
_____

Now turn it around. Infuse the situation with God's love. What are you discerning about the situation or person? _____

_____
_____
_____
_____
_____
_____
_____
_____

How should you pray for and bless the person or situation? _____

_____
_____
_____
_____

# Day #29 – The *"My Behavior Condemns Me"* Lie
## By Chris Glatzel

Our thoughts may not condemn us, but what if we act on those thoughts? Does our behavior condemn us?

We probably all have those friends that are controlled by addictions in some way. I have been known to consume a whole cheesecake, or the 1lb bag of m&m's. I don't ever hear that preached about, but there are a few special addictions that occasionally get mentioned from the pulpit.

For example, I had a neighbor that struggled with alcoholism. She worked hard for a few years on being sober, then she relapsed. It was such a disappointment to me. But after she was sober again for a while, she made it clear that even though the alcohol had a grip on her in the past and it was still a temptation in the present, she was fighting to be free. And that the whole time her trust in God hadn't wavered. Her heart was after God, so is she condemned?

We sometimes mess up, with what we say or do, and immediately the accuser is there to say there is no hope. But when Jesus was asked to condemn the woman caught in adultery, He simply said, I don't condemn you, don't do it again. She knew she was wrong, and perhaps she even messed up a few times again. But I believe she was on an upward spiral. When we add self-hatred or condemnation to our decision making we have the opposite reaction. We spiral downward.

> *But whenever someone turns to the Lord, the veil is taken away. For the Lord is the Spirit, and wherever the Spirit of the Lord is, there is freedom. So all of us who have had that veil removed can see and reflect the glory of the Lord. And the Lord – who is the Spirit –*

> *makes us more and more like him as we are changed into his glorious image. (2 Corinthians 3:16-18, NLT)*

As we walk with God, He is making us more and more like Him. I've often heard it said that life is a journey, not a destination. One wrong turn isn't going to change your whole life's trajectory if you don't let it. We are set on a path and if we are headed in a wrong direction then we need to do what the Bible tells us to do, "Repent", which is simply a military term that means to do an about face. Change direction if you need to.

Sometimes when I mess up, I think about people like Peter, one of Jesus' disciples. Boy, did he really mess up. When Jesus was arrested, he became so afraid that he would be arrested too, that he lied about even knowing Jesus. But in John 21, we see Jesus restoring Peter and reestablishing a bond of love with him. Making a wrong choice, even a really bad choice doesn't mean that the bond of love between you and Jesus has been broken beyond all repair.

We need to trust in the fact that His work on the cross accomplished our forgiveness and accept that forgiveness and His love. It's only then that we can become free to love ourselves, as He loves us. I personally think that addictions and bad behaviors are a result of not knowing what God thinks about us and not really believing that God loves us to our core.

Freedom comes from recognizing and dealing with the lies that we've been talking about in this book, and forgiving those that might have wounded us at the point when the lies rushed in.

So, our behaviors can only condemn us if they also become our heart attitude of hopelessness and helplessness. They do not condemn us when we RECEIVE the love and forgiveness He offers and walk toward Him.

What addiction do you run toward instead of God? _____
_____

Is there a lie you are believing about yourself that is feeding this addiction? What is it? _____
_____
_____

Who do you need to forgive for causing the wound that introduced that lie?
_____

Do you truly love yourself? _____

**FORGIVE:** *God, I chose to forgive* _____ *for making me feel like* _____.

**REWIND:** *I reject the lie that* _____
_____

**REST:** *I accept the truth that* _____
_____

**RESPOND:** Ask Father God to show you what He thinks of you. Write that here: _____
_____
_____
_____
_____
_____
_____
_____
_____

# Day #30 – The *"I Am a Victim of My Circumstances"* Lie
## By Chris Glatzel

We've talked a lot about wounds and issues that have impacted us and introduced lies into our lives. But not everyone moves past the wounded stage. They are perpetual victims who feel powerless to change themselves. They can easily see who is to blame for their issues and problems, but they never move past that point and deal with anything.

Ever since I've dealt with the spirit of shame, I've also seen this other tagalong spirit - victim. It all goes hand in hand. If shame has told you that you are no good, you will never amount to anything, your thoughts aren't valid, you are worthless and despicable, then it makes sense that its extremely hard to look at your actions and not feel depressed or even worse. So, the obvious thing to do is to never look at your own actions as being your fault. You think it's understandable why you can't deal with life while you're in a pit of despair. If conviction says you did something wrong, you need to clean up your mess, then shame says you *are* something wrong and there is no hope of you ever getting right.

Our inborn self-preservation response is to put the blame and responsibility outside ourselves onto someone else. If we were punished harshly as children, we will do almost anything to deflect blame away from ourselves. Or perhaps it is a response to never having to deal with the consequences of your own actions. No one has ever held you accountable, so nothing is ever your fault.

It was so and so's fault that I couldn't change things, they wanted to do that, so I went along. I was born in the wrong season. I had an accident and it messed up my life. Everything in life is blamed on outside circumstances.

None of it is our personal responsibility. We weren't strong enough to say no. Or, strong enough to know the right boundaries, so we have no borders.

People can easily take advantage of victims because they have no back bone, no internal compass. They've given themselves over to letting every random circumstance dictate their lives. Maybe that's why battered women find it difficult to leave their abusive situations, because they've believed all the lies that say they are worthless, and that they have no voice.

On the other side of this are people who tend to have no boundaries in other people's lives. They take what they want, they cross all kinds of inappropriate lines, and they have no sense of responsibility to clean up their own messes.

If you identify with feeling like you are a victim without the power to change anything, think about this verse from Psalm 10.

> *But you, God, see the trouble of the afflicted; you consider their grief and take it in hand. The victims commit themselves to you; you are the helper of the fatherless. (Psalm 10:14, NIV)*

Just because you have been a victim in the past doesn't mean you have permission to stay there. You have a God who is going to help you past that. I have a friend who likes to tell me, that if I'm continuing in negative behavior that I'm getting something out of it. Maybe attention, maybe a feeling of justification for my failings. But there is a greater truth out there than what is keeping me in a negative place and that's what we all need to strive for. That greater truth is that instead of being a victim, God declares me 'more than a conqueror'.

> *No, in all these things we are more than conquerors through Him who loved us. (Romans 8:37, BSB)*

So, what's the answer for the victim spirit? The answer is to get rid of its buddy - shame. If you identify with feeling like you are the victim of your circumstances, pray this after me. *"I see you spirit of shame. Get out of my life immediately and permanently. In Jesus name. I choose to no longer agree with you or any of your lies, including the lie that I have no power, and that I am a victim. I receive the truth of what Father God says about me. I am His child, and I am His favorite. He's delighted with how he made me and all the plans he has for my life. All my mess ups will never separate me from His amazing love. I choose to see myself the way He sees me, and let my life follow His direction instead of letting it be dictated by circumstances. I invite the Holy Spirit to fill me, and know that as I follow Him the fruits will grow. Love Joy Peace, Patience, Goodness and Self Control. Amen.*

**FORGIVE:** *God, I choose to forgive myself for using the excuse of being a victim. I choose to forgive _____ for _____*

*which caused the wounds and lies of _____*

*to enter my heart.*

**REWIND:** *I reject the lies of _____*

*and that I am a victim and powerless to change myself.*

**REST:** *I accept the truth that You are healing those wounds and empowering me to move past my situation.*

**RESPOND:** How have you been acting like a victim? _____

_____

_____

_____

How will you turn that around and act on the truth that you are 'more than a conqueror in Christ Jesus'? _____

# Prologue

Writing this devotional has been an exercise in examining our own issues. It isn't always easy to be this vulnerable. And sometimes it is painful. But we want freedom from the lies that are keeping us stuck. And that's what we desire for you as well.

Working through this devotional is a great start. Continue forgiving yourself and others and identifying and rejecting the lies that have been introduced into your heart. Always agree with God's truth.

If you've enjoyed this devotional, consider leaving a review. Feel free to contact us with questions or comments at pennyprincesspress@gmail.com.

For more information about the authors their ministries and other works by them go to www.pennyprincesspress.com.

Other books by Sharon L Letson and Chris Glatzel:

When Life Hurts: Using Art to Process Difficult Emotions (coloring book)

The Hands of Jesus (picture book for younger children)

Books by Sharon L Letson:

Watch Over Me

Ordinary Extraordinary (picture book)

O Jerusalem, Jerusalem

The Seventh City

Orion's Song

Made in the USA
Middletown, DE
21 June 2019